Talk to Me Like I'm Someone You Love

NANCY DREYFUS, PSY.D.

JEREMY P. TARCHER/PENGUIN

a member of Penguin Group (USA) Inc. · New York

Talk to Me Like I'm Someone You Love

Relationship Repair in a Flash

Jeremy P. Tarcher/Penguin
Published by the Penguin Group

Penguin Group (USA) Inc., 375 Hudson Street, New York, New York 10014, USA • Penguin Group (Canada), 90 Eglinton Avenue East, Suite 700, Toronto, Ontario M4P 2Y3, Canada (a division of Pearson Penguin Canada Inc.) • Penguin Books Ltd, 80 Strand, London WC2R 0RL, England • Penguin Ireland, 25 St Stephen's Green, Dublin 2, Ireland (a division of Penguin Books Ltd) • Penguin Group (Australia), 707 Collins Street, Melbourne, Victoria 3008, Australia (a division of Pearson Australia Group Pty Ltd) • Penguin Books India Pvt Ltd, 11 Community Centre, Panchsheel Park, New Delhi—110 017, India • Penguin Group (NZ), 67 Apollo Drive, Rosedale, Auckland 0632, New Zealand (a division of Pearson New Zealand Ltd) • Penguin Books (South Africa), Rosebank Office Park, 181 Jan Smuts Avenue, Parktown North 2193, South Africa • Penguin China, B7 Jiaming Center, 27 East Third Ring Road North, Chaoyang District, Beijing 100020, China

Penguin Books Ltd, Registered Offices: 80 Strand, London WC2R 0RL, England

Most Tarcher/Penguin books are available at special quantity discounts for bulk purchase for sales promotions, premiums, fund-raising, and educational needs. Special books or book excerpts also can be created to fit specific needs. For details, write Penguin Group (USA) Inc. Special Markets, 375 Hudson Street, New York, NY 10014.

Library of Congress Cataloging-in-Publication Data
Dreyfus, Nancy.
Talk to me like I'm someone you love : relationship repair in a flash / Nancy Dreyfus.
p.   cm.
ISBN 978-0-399-16200-8
1. Couples—Psychology.   2. Married people—Psychology.   3. Couples therapy.   4. Marriage counseling.
5. Man-woman relationships.   I. Title.
HQ801.D762   2009   2009042763
646.7'8—dc22

Printed in the United States of America
7   9   10   8   6

BOOK DESIGN BY AMANDA DEWEY

ALWAYS LEARNING   PEARSON

To my daughter, Carly Raphael,
a constant reminder that no words
can match the love underneath.

Contents

30. When you won't communicate with me, I feel like I'm nothing to you.

31. I'm embarrassed to say that I don't even remember what I'm arguing with you about.

32. It's frightening to me that we see things so differently.

33. I'm starting to disappear. It feels like there's no space for me.

34. It's hard admitting I might be wrong.

35. I'm afraid that if I say I'm sorry, you'll make everything all my fault.

36. Do you hate me?

37. I think I'm supposed to know how to do this, but honestly, I have no idea.

38. I feel like a total and complete idiot.

IV. TAKING RESPONSIBILITY 119

39. I can see that I've missed the point. Please give me another chance.

40. I can see that my anger has been destructive and that I've really hurt you.

41. I realize I'm overreacting. Can you give me a minute to get sane again?

42. I know I've been relentless. I can understand why you'd want to get away from me.

43. I know I haven't made it very safe for you. Please don't give up on me.

44. You are not being crazy. I can see why you'd be upset with me.

45. You are so upset, I probably don't fully understand my impact on you. Please tell me—I want to understand.

46. I'm probably sounding like a parent right now, and I can appreciate that it's a turnoff.

47. I was just reacting to you as if you were my mother, and I know that you're not.

48. I was just reacting to you as if you were my father, and I know that you're not.

49. I'm probably [sounding . . . looking . . . carrying on] like your mother right now, and I can appreciate how [frightening . . . disturbing . . . annoying] that must be for you.

50. I'm probably [sounding . . . looking . . .

carrying on] like your father right now, and I can appreciate how [frightening . . . disturbing . . . annoying] that must be for you.

51. I'm probably acting like _____ right now, and I can appreciate how disturbing that might be for you.

52. I'm probably acting like _____ right now, and I can appreciate how disturbing that might be for you.

V. GIVING INFORMATION

53. I don't feel heard.

54. I know I'm pretty shut down right now . . . but I promise I'll be back.

55. I'm in knots. I'm afraid to tell you my truth, and it's horrible feeling that I have to humor you.

56. I beg you to hear this as me truly wanting you to register my feelings—*not* as an attack on you.

57. You don't have to agree with me, but it hurts when you don't take me seriously.

58. You didn't do anything wrong. I know it's my own craziness—trust me to get through it.

59. When you are so intense, it's hard to take in what might be valid about what you are saying.

60. You are taking up so much space right now, it feels like there is no room for me.

61. Your behavior embarrassed me. I'm trying to tell you, not to make you feel bad, but so I can feel close to you again.

62. Your behavior was threatening to me. I'm trying to tell you about it, not to make you feel bad, but so I can feel safe with you again.

63. It feels like I can do no right by you.

VI. GETTING CLARIFICATION

64. When you treat me this way, it feels like you don't respect me. Is that true?

65. When you say things like that, it sounds like you are thinking of ending our

relationship. Is that what you really mean?

66. What can I say that would make you feel understood?

67. Tell me the truth—am I responding in the way you need me to right now?

68. Are you in the space to talk?

69. You seem so [prickly . . . defensive . . . enraged] that I feel pulled to do or say anything to calm you down. Is that what you really want?

70. I can absolutely see why you'd be annoyed with me, but can you give me some sign that we're still friends?

71. It would mean a lot to me if you could just repeat back to me what you think I'm trying to get across.

74. I know what I said was hurtful. I truly didn't mean it and would do anything to take it back.

75. I'm sorry that I've been acting as if everything's all your fault.

76. I feel embarrassed about how I spoke to you.

77. Please—can you forgive me?

78. Even though I've been arguing my position like a crazy person, I now see where your point of view makes sense.

79. I'm sorry I made such a big deal out of something so unimportant.

80. You have no idea how much I regret the direction I took this in. I'm really sorry.

81. I'm so sorry I couldn't hear you sooner.

82. I'm sorry that I acted as if there was only my reality.

VII. APOLOGIZING 203

72. I'm sorry.

73. I know I've really hurt you. What can I do that would help you trust me again?

VIII. LOVING 233

83. Right now, I'd do anything for you to know how much I love you.

84. I love you. And despite how it looks, I don't want our relationship to be a fight.

85. You don't have to be miserable to get me to take you seriously. Talk to me like I'm a friend who wants to do right by you.

86. I am not _____, who hurt you in the past. I am _____, who loves you now.

87. I am not _____, who hurt you in the past. I am _____, who loves you now.

88. I am not _____, who left you in the past. I am _____, who isn't going anywhere without you.

89. You are precious. And you deserve to be treated that way.

90. I love you and can't stand seeing you so unhappy.

91. I know I sounded like a maniac, but my love for you is still and deep.

92. I love you. I hate fighting. Can't we just hug?

93. I treasure you.

IX. MAKING UP 261

94. I can see how upset you are, and I feel terrible.

95. It would mean a lot if you could just say, "I'm sorry." Or do or say something that shows me that you care about what happened.

96. I'm worried that there's no space to make it better between us.

97. We need a new perspective. Let's take a break and each get clearer about what really matters here. Okay?

98. I would love it if we could just be quiet and hold each other.

99. I feel really crummy about what happened. Could we just make up?

100. I want to hug you, and I'm not sure I am welcome. May I come closer?

101. I forgive you completely. It never happened.

102. I want to make love—but only if you are liking me.

103. I'd love it if we could go slow.

104. I want to make love with you, too, but first I need to ask you something—and please don't hate me for asking—have you been avoiding conflict with me all day so that tonight doesn't get derailed?

105. When we are out of sync, you act like something is very wrong. Nothing's wrong—we just need to get back in sync . . .

106. When you give me the message that you think I'm just a guy "looking to get laid," it feels like you don't see me.

107. I know I behaved badly, but I don't want to have sex just to make it up to you. Can we clear things first?

108. I'm making up right now that you are feeling sexually deprived. My pattern is to make love to keep you from being upset with me. Let's do it differently this time.

109. I know you like to verbally process what's going on in our relationship first—but right now, if we could just touch each other, it could help me be more present with you.

110. I would love to share a sexual fantasy I have with you and I want it to bring us closer.

111. It's true. I'm not in a space to be sexual right now. Still, I love you and don't want you to make more of it than there really is (i.e., like this is the beginning of the end!) . . . Okay?

112. I'm terrified of pressuring you, but I'm worried that if we keep ignoring that we haven't made love in forever, we'll be past the point of no return. Talk to me about it . . . That's all I ask.

113. I'm thinking that you're thinking that I should know what you are wanting right now. I wish I did, honey, but I don't.

114. I'm out of words, and maybe even you are, too. Please, just be with me.

XI. DEEPENING TRUST 315

Preface to the Third Edition

've been told by everyone I know in the publishing world—and anyone who "knows what publishing is like these days"—that being given the opportunity to expand and update one's book is, without a doubt, an increasingly rare and fortunate honor. To put it mildly, I feel incredibly honored, deeply grateful . . . and occasionally just plain giddy.

Yet as someone whose life has revolved around personal growth, this development, while dramatic in itself, feels more like the natural next step in a project that has been re-creating itself for more than two decades. A relationship rupture may indeed be repaired in a flash, but the journey to Selfhood is a lifelong trek. My hope is that the ideas in this book—which largely have to do with choosing transparency when things get tense—will, however slowly, continue to be absorbed into mainstream culture until the day that there is peace on earth. In the meantime, this new version reflects a few new flashes I have had regarding the maintenance of even friendlier relationships.

To appreciate where we are now, first a quick recap of *Talk to Me Like I'm Someone You Love*'s trajectory: The entire incident is detailed in the introduction, but I created the first "Flash Card for Real Life" in 1991 when I was rendered virtually mute in a difficult couples session with a verbally abusive wife who happened to remind me of my mother. I handed to her worn-down husband a scrap piece of paper upon which I had written, "Talk to me like I'm someone you love . . ." and whispered to my father look-alike, "Hold it up to her." The woman became flustered, then genuinely nice, and responded to her husband kindly. The rest is history.

Over the next two weeks, I compiled about forty handwritten messages with Magic Marker on lined notecards, bound them with a loose-leaf ring and asked a few clients to go experiment with their spouses (a word more common then than "partners"). In 1992 I had Kinko's print up a basic, no-frills set, shrink-wrapped with a loose-leaf ring taped to the bottom. My practice at the time was mostly women, and they would come back the week after being given a set and report, "My husband finally heard me!" (It seemed one of the most helpful cards in the deck, hands-down, was "*I don't feel heard.*")

I had no entrepreneurial vision, and never thought these cards would leave my office, until I was at a large family gathering where I playfully stopped two quibbling relatives with a flash card. This feat was observed by my brother-in-law at the time, Michael E. Gerber, small-business wizard and author of the best-selling E-Myth business books, who shouted out, "It's a book!" and encouraged me to go public. This was a totally foreign idea, so on a lark I started selling the shrink-wrapped version at a therapy seminar, where the idea was picked up by consciousness writer Meredith Gould for a blurb in what was then *New Age Journal*. More than three thousand requests to buy copies in less than a month led quickly to the first formal publication of fifty-five flash cards with a simple introduction, *Talk to Me*, in a mini-book by Celestial Arts/Ten Speed Press in 1993, and then a reprint in 1995.

By 2000, that version was out of print, and I was going through enough of my own marital challenges, enough so that until I got my own bearings, I recused myself from offering the world one more piece of relationship advice. Then in 2006, I curiously began to get a slew of requests for copies of *Talk to Me* and discovered that my Flash Cards for Real Life had been registered in the Global Ideas Bank and were featured in their compendium, *500 Ways to Change the World* (HarperCollins, 2006).

Through a series of synchronistic events, which would be hard to believe occurred in the same week I had heard about my formal recognition, two people I had done favors for years before (for which I expected no repayment) reappeared independently in my life—one now a search-engine expert and the other an intellectual property lawyer. The latter wanted to help me get my publishing rights back in my own hands, and the former wanted to educate me on the power of the Internet to get my ideas circulated. After more than a dozen other agents personally communicated to me that they loved my thinking but didn't want to involve themselves with a previously published book, Joelle Delbourgo had the foresight to see, instead, that this was a retread whose time had come.

Sara Carder, a Tarcher/Penguin editor with an amazingly good head on her shoulders, could see where annotation majorly enriched things, and suddenly we were heading toward one hundred flash cards, each with its own little essay. I was now being asked to come up with more than just the right words. I was being asked to make real to others what was becoming increasingly real to me: that the commonly assumed notion of "connecting" to another person was actually confusing matters, particularly in a time of conflict. Instead, I wanted to give readers the conviction that the main thing they needed to concern themselves with was staying connected to their own insides within their partner's force field.

At the same time I was finishing the manuscript for the original version of the book in your hands, I was also falling in love with a man who, unlike my ex-husband and the numerous other male mental health professionals who had thus far populated my life romantically and otherwise, was a relative newcomer to the world of conscious communication. Tim was straightforward, unpretentious, very loving and—making it all possible—curious about his own wiring. However, when we first met, he wasn't so sure that my insistence that the difference between "You're attacking me!" and "I feel attacked" was the difference between night and day was more than some clever therapeutic tactic.

The Universe was giving me a "golden opportunity" to learn how to relate to a man operating more like the men that the women in my practice were describing—easily flooded by my ever-available interpretations, sensitive to feeling managed, and new to the world of reflective listening. Before the first edition hit the stores, Tim had taken flash card #21: "*Right now, I don't need a lecture. I need your love*," crossed out "lecture," replaced it with "therapist," framed it and hung it over the bed within easy reach. Now I knew I was in trouble . . . I had to relate like a real person. I might even have to cut back on my use of the word "relate."

As this highly personal practicum began interfacing with theory, my professional work with couples, and all pre-existing notions of growth, I could see that my hard-won capacity to be "authentic" under any and all conditions had its drawbacks with a partner who wasn't always immediately and cheerfully oriented to providing me with a safe container in which to perfect my authenticity. In fact, this partner would have preferred I take golf lessons over working on improving one more communication skill. Nevertheless, this unexpected catalyst, whom I found myself quite drawn to, showed me my capacity to trigger defensiveness in another, and that simply holding him 127 percent responsible for his own reactivity made me feel pristine—but wasn't adding to anybody's happiness.

So, the mind-set with which I am approaching this updated edition isn't asking the Reader to dilute his or her truth—but to speak it with less intensity and with more awareness of one's partner's vulnerability. I'm just saying be aware of your partner's vulnerability—I'm not saying to make it the point of your compass. For instance, the first new flash card is #102: "*I want to make love—but only if you are liking me.*" Notice I'm starting with an invitation first—then the self-worthy boundary. Even a few years ago, I might have likely phrased it, "*When you don't feel friendly to me, it's hard to want to make love.*" That would have been a clear, honest, nonbelligerent and nonarguable statement definitely allowing the Sender to convey the state of her soul—but there would have been a hint of admonition to it. While the shift isn't dramatic or relevant to every single flash card, my newer writing feels a notch less assertive and a little softer and more inclusive. Flash card #103 turned out to be "*I'd love it if we could go slow,*" not "*I'd love it if we could slow down.*" Less assertion, more invitation . . . Feel the difference?

(And frankly, a few years ago, it would never have crossed my mind to even have sexually themed flash cards—primarily because I didn't have quite enough of the right field experience to play expert. And I had spent so much time just contemplating whether people would ever use the cards in a car [universally, a conflict hot spot!] . . . that by the time I might have started on bedrooms, I was done obsessing over one more logistical challenge regarding on-the-spot flash card procurement.)

The two new sections in *Talk to Me Like I'm Someone You Love* are X, "Making Love," and XI, "Deepening Trust." They emerged partly as a function of me simply being better able to personally navigate trickier relationship terrain. But they are also the result of the common feedback I got from readers telling me that while they were inspired experiencing how a flash card intervention could almost always redirect a depressing interaction, it was also true that simply reading the book was teaching them how to feel, think and connect more deftly on their feet without the actual card. And they wanted to know: was there a way to bring *Talk to Me*'s thinking into the realm where disconnects impact sexual dynamics (meaning just about always) and the realm where an apparent relationship rupture is but upstream from a far broader underlying distrust that's been muddying the whole relationship (meaning fairly frequently)?

So this incarnation opens up the field for using written messages, not just for your rupture du jour (flash card #1: *"This feels awful. Can we start again and really listen to each other?"*), but for the problem that's been simmering for a very long time (e.g., #112: *"I'm terrified of pressuring you, but I'm worried that if we keep ignoring that we haven't made love in forever, we'll be past the point of no return . . ."*). Or some kind of betrayal that's been outed, but definitely not vaporized (e.g., #123: *"I know you feel awful—but it's not enough. I need you to really, really know what it was like for me."*). In other words, I'm more explicit about putting your whole relationship on a healing path, and as Lao-tzu no doubt would have put it if he had been familiar with this book, a journey of a thousand miles can begin with a single flash . . .

Over the twenty years this project has been reconfiguring itself, it has been an interesting paradox that a profound healing journey could begin with a written message composed by neither you nor your partner. It has not infrequently been noted that I am encouraging people to be sincere and thoughtful—yet how can that be since I'm "giving them the lines"? I've grappled with this on a number of levels—and have come to an important discovery about the purpose of this book.

Talk to Me Like I'm Someone You Love is both first aid for a painful interaction and a manual for staying true to oneself when it might seem impossible. It can help make it safe for you to be transparent and let you speak from your heart without distracting voice tones. And it fortunately turns out that I totally lack the power to make you insincere. Because, appearances to the contrary, this book isn't really telling you what to say, after all. It is only giving you permission to remember who you really are . . . and trusting that you'll figure out how to take it from there.

Nancy Dreyfus, Psy.D.

Wynnewood, Pennsylvania

July 2012

Introduction

What you are holding in your hands is a very helpful, practical and sometimes magical tool that can move you and a loved one in a much kinder direction when you are stuck in an unhappy spiral of arguing, defensiveness or just ordinary terrible listening.

The idea behind this book is rooted in a piece of basic common sense: no matter what form the strain in your relationship is taking—be it jumping down each other's throats, nitpicking, walking on eggshells or endlessly revisiting an ancient grievance—it will be near impossible to begin to solve your problems if the energy between you and your partner feels more *unfriendly* than *friendly*. And as a psychotherapist specializing in couples therapy as well as the veteran of a twenty-year marriage, I have noticed something about the way words are used, or not used, to make this shift. If a couple is unable to make contact in a way that feels genuine, there are virtually no words that can fix what's wrong. Over and over, we can try to hammer our point home or make nice for the sake of peace . . . and over and over, no matter how articulate or forceful or even compliant we are, the longing for connection remains until it is, at least, recognized. Sometimes this is for twenty minutes . . . sometimes it is for years . . . sometimes, sadly, never. Whether it gets expressed directly or not, the continued experience of feeling unheard and unseen leads to rage. And I can assure you that few of us are exceptional at maintaining an atmosphere of friendly mutuality when we're feeling threatened.

I created *Talk to Me Like I'm Someone You Love* for couples (and sometimes parents and children) to transform unproductive, mean or just plain crummy interactions into moments of connection. I like to see this book as a first aid kit for swiftly generating goodwill and restoring intimacy in exchanges that have gone off course. It contains 101 of what I've come to call Flash Cards for Real Life—frank, non-defensive messages that have the power to quietly reverse the course of a difficult interaction by going right to the heart of "feeling connected." These messages work because one person has made the momentous choice to redirect the ongoing tension they are experiencing with another person from the *content* of the interaction—parenting, money, sex, how-could-you-have-forgotten-to-pick-up-the-prescription?, etc.—to the *context.* This is the real arena—how the two of you are treating each other in the moment.

In order to explain in more depth how this book works, let me tell you the story of how I came to create it. Over the years, I've worked with hundreds of couples as well as individuals in relationship, and watched the stunning ease with which partners get derailed in their attempts to connect and sustain connection. I've watched couples miss over and over again what marital researcher John Gottman, Ph.D., calls each other's "bids for connection." I've watched women explain in precise detail to their husbands what felt so off to them in their husbands' approach—and still not feel much closer at the end of this impassioned sharing. I concluded that an important key to repairing a rupture in connection was deepening levels of vulnerability. So I would coach or, ideally, inspire partners who were having an upset to drop down to a deeper level of internal sensing and share with their loved one when they were feeling invisible, disrespected, lectured, belittled, invaded, bullied, shamed, unappreciated, ignored, unrelated to, trapped, humored or simply unheard.

Usually this defused tension considerably, particularly if both partners shared and both felt received by the other. Yet I also couldn't help but notice that this defusing of tension didn't always lead to a warm, tender feeling of emotional closeness. A couple might feel relieved that peace was being restored, that their partner was no longer upset with them, that, at last, their previous reactivity made some sense to their loved one. But it didn't always lead to a hug, either a physical one or an energetic one. Partners could get high marks in processing a conflict, and then go their separate ways and not really feel the special closeness they had hoped would emerge from their sincere clearing.

At a time when I was fascinated with the enormous gifts of intimate communication, as well as sensing some way that words weren't always enough, I had a couples session with one of the most critical wives and emotionally battered husbands I had ever worked with. Through what I can only call divine intervention, or perhaps God's peculiar sense of humor, the particular couple in my consulting room also happened to be sent from central casting to replay the roles of my parents. As I had witnessed countless times in my own childhood, this woman was unrelenting in her criticism of her increasingly inarticulate, emotionally withdrawn husband. I remember the wife smirking and faulting her husband for an "asinine" business decision. Quickly after, in what clinically would be called my "countertransference reaction," I felt myself go numb in the familiar way I did as a child. I was all but directionless as to how to proceed with my clients, and felt unusually incompetent as a therapist. More as a last resort than an intentional therapeutic act, I scribbled on a scrap piece of paper in my office, *Talk to me like I'm someone you love!* and whispered to the near-mute husband, "Hold it up to her."

The husband did this and within seconds the wife softened, truly startling both her husband and me when what came out of her mouth was, "I haven't been very nice, have I? . . . You deserve better from me." The husband sat straighter in his chair, embodying the self-respect his message carried. He didn't quite smile at her yet, but when he looked his wife in the eye, for the first time I had ever seen, it was without fear. *Within minutes*, the ancient power differential between the partners shifted, and a realer, gentler and strikingly more mutual connection began emerging in front of everyone's eyes. Soon the two of them were focusing on some decision they had to make regarding one of their kids. They looked like they were actual friends and equals.

Why These Flash Cards Work

I felt what I had witnessed was an answer to a prayer. There was some special power in a written message to heal a relationship rupture—but what was going on I wasn't exactly sure. Over the past decade, as I have worked with more and more couples (and have understood more about my own reactivity), I have come to understand it a bit more.

Let's start with a question. If being in a warm, intimate space with a loved one is so desirable, feels so good and is often the experience declared to be, arguably, the most wonderful feature of human existence, *why is it that so often even a very small thing can disrupt the good feeling between a couple and make it so hard to get back to it?* Why is it that even a minor disagreement, let alone a full-scale fight, can be so hard to repair? Why is it that sometimes your partner can genuinely say, "I'm sorry," and you can hear the words, know he or she means it, and still not feel as relaxed or safe with them as you did before they, say, interpreted a lost sales receipt as saying something "significant" about your lack of responsibility . . . or before you made a smart-ass remark that you thought was so witty, it wouldn't leave you partner feeling small and devalued—but it did . . . before you were questioned about something—almost anything—with "that tone" in your partner's voice?

Think of all the times you and a partner were happily anticipating a special evening, and by the time you got in the car and were heading for the restaurant, it was already less than relaxed between you. Consider Laura and Michael, who had been looking forward to going out to a ninth-anniversary dinner:

"We were supposed to have a special evening together, Michael, just the two of us—and you *had* to go run and answer your cell phone. [*pleadingly*] *It's our anniversary . . .*"

"Laura, we have the whole evening ahead of us. You *know* I want to be with you. I made the reservation weeks ago. [*mild irritation in his voice*] *Why do you have to focus on one little thing and ruin everything?*"

"*I've* ruined everything? I'm *only* telling you how I feel. If the plan is to be close tonight, do you think you could listen to how I feel? If you really cared about our evening, you never would have picked up the phone in the first place."

"Why don't you ask me *why* I picked up the phone—that might show caring about someone's feelings other than your own. Laura, you know how precarious things are between Terry and me at the office. Why can't you trust that I picked up the phone for a good reason?"

"But it's *always* a good reason. Why can't you simply appreciate how much it bothers me that we never seem to have time together without an interruption. It feels like you would rather win a point with Terry than just be with me."

"Now I'm irritated. Stop with the analysis, Laura. If you weren't so insecure, you could allow me taking one brief call without falling apart."

"Oh, really? If *you* weren't so insecure, you could hear the phone ring and not have to check whether your world was falling apart . . ."

Do couples therapists make house calls? How does a simple moment get so complicated? How could a well-intentioned romantic evening turn sour so fast? Why can't Laura stop pushing? Why can't Michael just see that she's hurt? Why is each so hell-bent on proving how insensitive the other is? Why is this downward spiral so hard to stop? We'll get back to Laura and Michael in a moment, but first a little background perspective to help make sense of their spiral.

For starters, feel into this idea: We are never upset for the reason we think. Allow yourself to consider where this statement might be true: *We are never upset for the reason we think.*

Many years ago, when I was staying with a friend who was having a party, I felt that she became unduly upset because I accidentally left my makeup case in a bathroom—a room she, admittedly, had asked be kept pristine. Inwardly I rolled my eyes and implied she was being an unreasonable taskmaster ("I mean, *get real*—it's just a makeup case . . . people keep makeup cases in bathrooms!"). Closer examination uncovered that I also: felt hurt that she didn't appreciate the clean-up job I did do; felt anxious that she was likely remembering all the other past times I had been less than impeccable; felt a bit depressed that this was happening at all, and wondered what it said about our relationship; and felt shame that she had made a simple, heartfelt request and I had screwed up. At one level, my eye-rolling and pointing to her rigidity were not unreasonable responses to her disdain—only they were defensive, masking an extensive emotional underground. And no doubt on her side, underneath her surface disapproval were feelings about not being taken seriously, feeling ridiculed by me and feeling disappointed that she couldn't just trust me to do what she asked.

Add to the picture that these underground feelings are almost always rooted in *still potent* unmet childhood needs—to be seen, heard, affirmed and treated as precious. I could have sincerely apologized for forgetting the makeup case, but that would have been inadequate, given that what my friend needed to hear was a deeper understanding of the meaning of the incident. Rightly or wrongly, some part of her felt not taken seriously and somewhat powerless with me. Even if I had made this empathic leap—a milestone in itself—how well could I have truly conveyed that empathy when a part of me was still feeling belittled by her focusing on an oversight, and not trusting that she could see my humanity coexisting with my more casual approach to housekeeping? If you think about it, it's amazing that any two people make it through any mid-range upset, let alone a full-blown fight. Sadly, this is why there is such an epidemic of relational discord on the planet, not to mention perpetual global warfare.

Let's go back to our anniversary couple, Laura and Michael. We can see how quickly two well-meaning people, who were looking forward to a romantic evening, can get off track. In the throes of their interaction it's apparent that a part of Laura is convinced Michael isn't as invested in their time together as she is, and interprets his taking the phone call as "evidence." Michael is hurt that Laura neither sees his good intentions nor seems interested in what is going on in his world. Michael cannot see that Laura is hurt and worried; Laura cannot see Michael's caring and need for her to understand that his concern with a work situation doesn't diminish his desire to be with her.

But from the "we are never upset for the reason we think" standpoint, a case could be made that Laura's hurt might be something far greater than Michael not focusing sufficiently on their time together, that Michael's behavior is, in fact, evidence of a more secret preexisting fear—*that she's not worth being given sustained attention in the first place.* It's this anxiety about her basic value—something far more fundamental than her value to Michael—that could well be fueling her relentlessness.

Furthermore, when Laura initially registered upset that he took the call, Michael didn't immediately respond, "Honey, I can totally see why you might have worried I was going to get all tied up with work on our anniversary—and you would have every reason in the world to be upset with me if I did that." This would have gotten everything back on track, not to mention establishing Michael as the most conscious male of the decade! Why? Because he would have given Laura what all of our wounded parts, and many of our healthy parts, crave—the experience we often didn't get enough of in childhood, the experience of *feeling felt*[*] by a loved one. If Laura had had enough of *feeling felt* when she was younger, she would have had the self-worth to experience the minor interruption by Michael as an annoyance, not a catastrophe. She might have acknowledged her annoyance playfully by saying something like, "Okay, buster, you can take the call, but for every minute on the phone you have to massage me for two minutes!" The annoyance is registered, and the energy stays friendly.

Ruptures between couples often get superficial healing because apologies and acknowledgments are offered, oftentimes sincerely ("You are right . . . I shouldn't have picked up the phone"), but they don't actually hit the mark. They don't leave an upset partner *feeling felt*, conveying a message that their being upset makes sense to the other. Often this has to do with

---

[*] "Feeling felt" is a formulation from spiritual teacher D. S. Barron's *There's No Such Thing as a Negative Emotion* (Outskirts Press, 2005).

Partner A acknowledging the impact of his or her behavior on Partner B, something far more meaningful than just acknowledging that the behavior itself was unwise. Let's not make Michael carry more of the responsibility here than is his. Laura didn't do her part in allowing herself to be better felt, such as sweetly expressing, "Listen, my anniversary-mate, could you just appreciate that your picking up the phone triggered me?" Because she didn't, we now have another unspoken issue in the space: I feel unimportant when you don't acknowledge your impact on me. Underneath that is another deeper secret fear: *there must be something wrong with me if I can't get the people who matter to me to see their effect on me . . . so I must not really matter.*

Michael can apologize all he wants and offer a stream of assurances, but he still doesn't have a clue that what's now percolating in Laura is far afield from the ostensible subject, allowing one-on-one time to be interrupted by a phone call. And, keep in mind, so far, we are just dealing with Laura's underground psychological terrain—and probably only a segment of it. Michael brings his own universe of preexisting wounds to the table: expectations of criticism, doubts of whether he can "get it right," worries of whether he can truly please a woman and pain that he is loved more for what he can give another than just for himself. And so on and so on . . .

But before I give you a bit more theory, let's go to the practicum. Let's revisit Laura and Michael's parting shots:

"But it's *always* a good reason. Why can't you simply appreciate how much it bothers me when we never seem to have time together without an interruption? It feels like you would rather win a point with Terry than just be with me."

"Now I'm irritated. Stop with the analysis, Laura. If you weren't so insecure, you could tolerate me taking one brief call without falling apart."

"Oh, really? If *you* weren't so insecure, you could hear the phone ring and not have to check whether your world was falling apart . . ."

Now imagine that one of our defensive duo happens to have a copy of this book, goes to page 22 and kindly holds up the flash card on that page: *"This feels awful. Can we start again and really listen to each other?"*

Imagine the sniping ceasing and the defensiveness gone. Perhaps they smile at each other a bit sheepishly, but their affection is real. Imagine the conversation about their evening out resuming, only this time with an infusion of tenderness and care.

Where only minutes before, Laura and Michael seemed headed for an achingly familiar downward spiral, we now hear things like, *"Thank you, sweetie,"* and *"I felt horrible thinking we had almost blown our evening"* and *"I melted when you held up that page."* We might even hear, *"I'm sorry, I wasn't listening,"* *"I'm so sorry I gave you a hard time."* Wordlessly the couple beams at each other. *"I like it when we remember that we like each other."*

Whether we are talking about Laura and Michael or the couple that first moved me to scribble a written note in my office—or the couple living under your roof—most intimate ruptures involve our ancient personal struggle to be heard, felt and recognized. Whether you and your partner are aggressively attacking each other or unconsciously avoiding each other, everyone's sense of self is on the line. From this perspective, reconciliation requires a letting go of our self-protective mask as much as our grievances, and it is here that the written word is so useful as a peace initiative.

In such a situation, the act of refraining from making the next uncharitable remark is in itself no small thing. To then go through the effort of finding and offering an appropriate flash card is often experienced by both parties as a true relational act, and a very tender moment. In an instant, the Sender has signaled to the Receiver:

- that he has given up some of his defenses, not the least of which is pride;
- that she is now making the relationship matter more than her position;
- that he didn't enjoy holding on to his negativity as much as his partner feared that he did;
- that she really wishes to be closer; and
- that magically, he has become a more giving person than he was a few minutes ago. The flash card, after all, is a gift.

When a couple is in a reactive mode, verbal statements that could theoretically move the two of you in a more peaceful direction get drowned out in the face of the wounded person's need to hang on to the affront he or she feels to his dignity. Talk is cheap—it's what we do with each other all day long. In the midst of battle, combatants are usually too busy thinking up their next remark to even *hear* a conciliatory gesture.

More to the point, a verbal message is often not appreciated as sincere because of the tentative or possibly sardonic tone of voice in which it is delivered. Voice tone—real or imagined—carries enormous weight. If the speaker's tonality isn't perfectly angelic—which it often isn't in the limbo between resentment and letting go—it is not uncommon for the Receiver to focus on some strand of the gesture that could possibly lack conviction, like a faintly exasperated vibe that might typically accompany the words *"All right already!"* This could lead the offended party to discount the peacemaker and take further offense at the latter's insincerity. "Don't think you can shut me up so easily!" is the battle cry of our insincerity detector.

This is where written messages really seem to have an edge. The novelty of the visual format gives them an excellent chance of being received and appreciated. Knowing this gives the Sender the courage to make the first move, overcoming the very human resistance to being the one to "give in." Likewise, the written form neutralizes a certain level of worry about being heard and about being taken seriously.

One doesn't have to be an emotional intelligence genius to appreciate that the offering of a repair message implies some emotional risk, and with that awareness, even the most generic of messages (*"I'm sorry"*) are almost universally experienced by recipients as sincere and, surprisingly, quite personal.

When couples are feeling victimized and defensive, locked into what psychotherapist Harriet Lerner, Ph.D., termed "the dance of anger" in her book of the same name, the emotional relevance and resonance of any particular message is both calming and bonding. But keep in mind that *the whole transaction itself* is a potentially sacred gift. This is because the person offering the written repair message is introducing two vital ingredients into the combat zone: giving and receiving. These are the fundamental building blocks of love, and as such, the whole transaction piercingly reminds disconnected partners of what they have been wanting to regain in the first place. The simple act of one partner giving something—in this case, the flash card—and then the other partner receiving it is rehearsal for sane love. It reminds you and your partner that something feels far better than fighting, and that the two of you, indeed, are capable of producing that something.

How to Use This Book

Before using these Flash Cards for Real Life in the trenches, it's a good idea to read through them all. Some may evoke a pang of recognition or appreciation ("Boy, that would have been handy last week when . . ."). In most relationships, what would have been handy a week ago will almost certainly be useful tomorrow. Some of the messages will be thoughts that you may have never thought to share before. Some will feel more "you" than others. Just allow yourself to take in this universe of repair possibilities. On the page opposite each ready-to-flash message, I have included some field notes on the particular message and some suggestions as to when its use might be optimal. Just by reading the flash cards and field notes, you are majorly expanding your response repertoire.

The messages in this book are divided into nine categories to assist you in finding the right tone and optimal words for whatever uncomfortable or painful encounter you happen to find yourselves in: *I. Shifting Gears, II. Setting Limits, III. Feeling Vulnerable, IV. Taking Responsibility, V. Apologizing, VI. Giving Information, VII. Getting Clarification, VIII. Loving and IX. Making Up.* Imagine you are stuck in a combative stance and are somewhat motivated to move in a kinder direction. (I say "somewhat" because that's usually the case initially; the messages are designed to move you toward wholeheartedness.) If you do not have a pre-designated message to go to, scan the list of categories in the table of contents and let yourself gravitate toward the section that seems to match your current emotional climate. Feeling intimidated by your partner might lead you to *Setting Limits*; feeling exposed and defensive might lead you to *Feeling Vulnerable* and feeling confused and worried about what your partner seems to be suggesting might make *Getting Clarification* a good place to start. And so on. Please keep in mind that the indexing is understandably subjective, and the "perfect message" may turn out to be not what you'd initially suspect.

If truth be told, the indexing of the statements was the most challenging aspect of conceptualizing *Talk to Me Like I'm Someone You Love*. It's not just that the interpretation of the messages is fairly subjective—it's that even objectively speaking, each message could be reasonably placed in several of the categories.

For instance, the flash card "I can see that my anger has been destructive and that I've really hurt you" was placed in section IV, *Taking Responsibility.* And this makes sense; the Sender would be taking responsibility for his or her impact on the Receiver. But at the same time, a case could be made for putting this message in the *Feeling Vulnerable* section, since when we take ownership of our own stuff it absolutely puts us in a vulnerable position. We have no idea whether our vulnerability will be received compassionately or will be an opportunity for our partner to *really* let us know how much we've hurt them. There is an implicit "I'm sorry" embedded in "I can see that my anger has been destructive . . ." and for similar reasons, another case could be made for placing the exact same flash card in the *Apologizing* section.

Furthermore, virtually *any* message in the entire book could fall under the heading *Feeling Vulnerable,* because the very act of leaving the combat zone and indicating "I'm putting down arms and showing you how much I'd rather be closer to you" is an act of exceptional vulnerability in itself, and of potential rejection if not well received. Likewise, the very act of offering a flash card is a move toward *Shifting Gears* and frequently one in the direction of *Making Up,* given that your partner will almost always be quite appreciative that one of you had the gumption to redirect things in a more humane manner. Similarly, almost any message is a form of *Giving Information* of an interpersonal, if not intimate, nature. And bringing things full circle, the very act of proffering the flash card is a *Loving* act, even if the specific language isn't particularly affectionate. "I hate feeling I have to walk on eggshells around you," from the *Setting Limits* section, isn't what you'd find on your average Hallmark card, but the mere act of quietly sharing this sentiment with your partner totally carries the powerful meta-message: "I want to feel safe with you"—and embedded in that message is yet another unspoken message: "It's scary getting close to you when I don't feel safe . . . and how I wish I were feeling closer to you." Most people would be very happy to get a Hallmark card from a loved one that said that. And they'd probably melt getting it.

All this being said, there actually is some comprehensible structure to the ordering of the flash cards, and my guess is that reading them, you'll get a feel for the logic that caused me to place a card in one section and not in another. I am taking the time, though, to acknowledge the idiosyncratic and un-pin-downable aspect of all this, so that you, the user, will not get hung up on using or not using a message because, say, you are on the road to *Apologizing* and the message that draws you happens to be in some other section. Or because your particular situation defies both my partial vision of things and the unique ways you and your beloved are hardwired.

While offering a message is usually more important than perfecting it, some moments do call for original messages. One woman reported turning a miserable interaction around when she wrote to her husband: *I don't really hate you. I got so mad when you told me I had to cancel the party because planning the party felt like an act of devotion toward you.* Creating your own message can be a beautiful way to honor yourself, your relationship and your commitment to sanity. To this end, a number of blank pages are provided at the end of this book.

· · ·

Over the years, as I have presented the concept of Flash Cards for Real Life, people sometimes question me on the user-friendliness of the whole idea. Typically I get, "How am I supposed to go look up a message and use it when I am triggered? It feels klunky . . . and it takes time!" Toward this end, I spent years contemplating how the indexing and mobility of the set could be maximally functional. But recently I have rethought this. If the Magic Communication Elf instantly put the perfect message in your hands, believe me, something would be lost. The point isn't to just calm your partner . . . it is to create a lucid interval in which you *consciously* shift gears and choose to be in your right mind over your reactive one. You *should* be part of making this happen and it *should* take a little time and effort on your part.

Rarely do you leave Starbucks or the ATM machine because two people unfortunately happen to be in line in front of you. No, you wait for your latte or for your money. If you know where the set is (not an insignificant point, and the reason why in a perfect world you should each have your own set), finding a relevant message takes far less time than the order and delivery of your latte. This is *your relationship,* for goodness' sake, and it should be worth the effort!

So here's the truth: it is less important that this gift in your hands be "user-friendly" than that *"the user be friendly."*

The other question I've heard a lot is: "What should I do if my partner is not open to using these flash cards?" It may be that one person will be enthusiastic about trying the repair messages in this book and the other will prefer to just make skeptical—even undermining—comments like "It's too contrived" or "dumb" or "We communicate so well, why would you ever think we need something like this?" I suggest that, when the occasion arises, the more willing partner simply offer a conciliatory message (for example, *"I can see that I've missed the point. Please give me another chance"*). Then, without fanfare, both of you can note the results. Your partner will likely be more open to these Flash Cards for Real Life once they've sampled their healing power.

I would add that some initial self-consciousness in using this guidebook to intimacy is not unusual. *Any* intimate gesture can be thwarted by anticipated awkwardness. The spirit of *Talk to Me Like I'm Someone You Love* is the willingness to do something that might feel a drop uncomfortable for the sake of mutual healing. Willingness itself is a loving thing. And the more the message reflects your truth, the more comfortable you are going to be with it.

Finally, I encourage you to experiment, in particular, with the title message of the set "Talk to me like I'm someone you love." It is an extremely healing statement and you'll hear more about it in the field notes on page 71. Consider, too, that in the midst of any real power struggle, the willingness to offer any heartfelt message implies "Come on, let's talk to each other like we really love each other." The messages only work because they tap into what we've been groping for all along—a shared awareness that the bond between us is so much more fundamental than our differences.

I hope that using *Talk to Me Like I'm Someone You Love* inspires you to forever trust your own insides to heal any relationship problem. I wish you the peace that comes from transforming unhappiness and the joy that comes from finding out how loving you really are.

PART I

Shifting

Gears

The flash cards in this particular grouping are straightforward acknowledgments that your interaction is not going well, and that the Sender is offering an opportunity for the two of you to pivot in a better direction. Many are calls for less reactivity and more attuned listening; a few are requests for some time-limited personal space. But the basic message of all of them is that what is going on right now is not good, and one of you is asking for something different.

The particular messages are relatively unspecific in terms of the emotional content attached to them (i.e., "I'm feeling intimidated" or "You're being pushy"), yet they have demonstrated time and again that they can freshen a stale, unkind or otherwise off-track interaction *precisely because* one person is willing to go inside and tell the truth about something they feel is needed in the moment.

These messages will get you on the road of developing a more broad-based trust in the power of your own inner awareness to transform something unattractive into something beautiful. You might even start by simply imagining what could happen by flashing one of these messages to your partner. Whether you begin in reality or fantasy, you will be organically building your own model of *how to access friendliness underneath the often compelling appearance of un-friendliness.*

I.

This feels awful. Can we start again and really listen to each other?

Though there were a few contenders, this deceptively simple message became the book's lead flash card for a reason. It is a very powerful intervention because, first of all, it tells the Receiver something that I can almost promise you is out of his or her awareness—that you also are not exactly enjoying the proceedings. What a notion. Think about it—when *you* are experiencing your partner in any way as difficult—and this could run the gamut from "just not getting it" to downright perverse—are you also thinking, "I'm sure Marty isn't enjoying this any more than I am"? No, you are probably not thinking this. In fact, it can even feel like Marty *is* enjoying whatever "this" is. So when you present this flash card to your co-weary partner, it is almost guaranteed to quickly "de-enemy-ize" you in their eyes and surprise them with the awareness that in this unpleasant, even adversarial, moment, you are *both feeling the same thing*: a distaste for what is going on.

The "really listen to each other" piece is also its own gift. The Sender is saying the greatest thing: "I know neither of us has been listening very well—and that includes me, sweetheart—and it is worth it to me to roll up my sleeves and do the thing that we both know needs to happen to turn this misery around: really get ourselves out of the way and hear each other. I'm up for it . . . you game?"

This is an extremely helpful flash card. The only caution I would use in regard to it is to choose a more self-responsible message acknowledging your own poor listening if, in fact, your partner actually has been relatively non-defensive, and the "we" in "Can we start again . . ." should be crossed out and replaced with an "I," who really wants to listen better to a certain "you."

2.

I know I'm being defensive. Can you say this in a less charged way so I can feel safe with you?

Even defensiveness, you shall see, has never really been the Problem. It is *unacknowledged* defensiveness that has been the killer in just about every crummy interaction you have ever had. The moment, though, that one of you takes ownership of your defensiveness, notice the extraordinary amount of Presence this brings into the room. To say, "I know I'm being defensive" means making the monumental shift from showing up as a reactive person mindlessly hitting, slamming or withholding the ball, to showing up as a sane, self-aware person with a high-level capacity to make tracking his insides a priority. Once this "Inner Tracker" reveals himself through this flash card, I can say with some assurance that the person on the receiving end will immediately get calmer. I can say this because, time and again in my work with couples, in the end it turns out that the person behaving in this allegedly "charged" manner was doing so precisely because she did not trust that there was a Someone across the way who was truly receiving her.

In the meantime, a Someone who is tracking his own defensiveness qualifies as a Someone you can trust because, no longer putting energy into protecting himself, he has energy available to listen. Moreover, in acknowledging his own defensiveness, he is communicating something major—that he is willing to own up to what happens to be True. The Sender, after all, is not telling the Receiver to be quiet. He is both inviting her to express herself in a way that will make it easier for her to be heard, and telling her he wants to feel safe with her. A very good deal for both parties.

This card originally started out saying, ". . . Can you say this in a *gentler* way so I can feel safe with you?" But it turned out that female recipients, in particular, felt sort of put down by being seen as not-gentle—which brought another whole level of defensiveness into the mix ("*So now you see me as cold and hard, is that it?*"). This is in support of a more general point: when you want to feel safer with someone, you don't have to get them to see how badly they are behaving. Just tell them you want to feel safer with them.

3.

I wish you could
hear this as me saying
"yes" to myself—not
"no" to you.

The reason we don't have a flash card in this book that just says, "Please don't take this personally," is because it would be a wasted card. Almost no one knows how to not take it personally.

If Marjorie wants fifteen more minutes on the phone with her girlfriend, when Paul is ready to watch the DVD . . . or Marjorie is ready to watch the movie and Paul needs fifteen minutes to check his e-mail . . . or one of them wants to meditate or go to sleep or, God forbid, finish a gripping mystery when the other wants to make love . . . it's a sure recipe for the other person to feel personally diminished or rejected or simply that they don't matter all that much to their partner. People who were severely neglected in childhood or had extremely self-absorbed parents can, frankly, have a hard time making the distinction between "yes" to myself and "no" to you. But even the sturdier among us can feel depreciated by a partner's choice, and this flash card is meant to soften that disappointment. Relationships provide endless forced-choice moments when conflicting agendas and/or realities require us to disappoint someone we love. You have worked tirelessly to land an impossible-to-schedule appointment with a highly desirable potential client. And later that night your partner informs you that he set up, at the exact same time, a medical appointment that he wants you to attend with him. Often you'll cancel the client, of course, but there are those times when the medical condition is routine enough—and the consequences of canceling the client feel extreme enough—that you will be truly torn. Your partner will take it personally. A partner with years of personal growth work will likely still take it personally, but at least know that they are doing this. A partner who doesn't take it personally has reached Enlightenment. Short of that, we recommend this flash card.

4.

All I want is for you
to listen to me with
an open heart.

When it comes to chronic relationship conflict, underneath everything you have been trying to explain, argue for or, for that matter, avoid with your partner is this one wish: please—just take in what's going on with me *with interest and without judgment*. I may want something that you don't want . . . I may see something entirely different from how you see it . . . but please, see that I am not a loony tune. If you could just hear how it is for me in my skin, you'd see how my feelings or behavior make sense . . . and that is what I need from you right now.

Notice how the language here—"*All I want is for you to listen . . .*"—suggests that you are only asking for one small, reasonable thing. In reality, however, what you are asking for may be reasonable, but it is by no means small. What you are asking for is to be understood and accepted as you are. Make no mistake—the Sender of this card is asking for Everything and, because of this, will need to possess of him- or herself a fair amount of confidence in their self-worth. For many of the flash cards, the words work alone, but this is a case where the request is so big that any accompanying energetic ambivalence on the part of the Sender (i.e., "I'm not 100 percent sure that I deserve what I am asking for") will likely keep the Receiver's guarded heart resistant. But if the Sender truly believes she is worth being listened to—and is not also demanding that her partner do more than take her seriously—it will be the former's consciousness of self-worth that will inspire her partner to let down his guard and listen to her freshly.

While you might want openheartedness around everything and anything, this flash card is recommended for situations where your partner seems particularly threatened that taking in your reality will seriously undermine his. He felt totally ignored by you the night before when you were presumably going to have some time together but ended up lingering for most of the evening at a neighbor's home or felt undermined by your reversing a parenting decision of his. You want him to understand that you were actually offering life-saving advice to the neighbor or that you were attempting to shield your child from unanticipated humiliation. His openheartedness will be more openhearted if, once you get the floor, you are sure he first gets that you understand his pain and the graciousness of his renewed willingness to listen.

Good to remember: hearts are forever opening and closing. An open heart has only opened one more time than it has closed. That's it . . . *only one more time.*

5.

I am upset. This doesn't mean that you are a bad person . . . It means that if you could just listen, I would feel incredibly loved.

This is a truth about relationships: though we can be oblivious to our partner's upset over something we have done, we can't *stand* it when our partner is upset with us.

In her classic parenting book *You Can Postpone Anything But Love* (Ambassador Press, 1985), Randy Rolfe makes the profound point that in any communication we hear the most abstract message first. This means: if your partner is agitated that you are not dressed for the wedding yet and is frantically updating you on traffic conditions on the Long Island Expressway, you are not particularly taking in messages about time management, wedding etiquette or, frankly, even his panic about being late. You mostly just hear, "Steve is upset with me."

With this flash card's "I *am* upset," you immediately validate your partner's reality and, at the same time, let them see that your upset is limited—not something that is spiraling endlessly into outer space. As children many of us received the message from our parents when they were upset with us that we were somehow bad and therefore less deserving of love—and we didn't know if and when it would stop. Now that we are adults, it is still a rare person who can see their partner upset about something they have done and not feel even a little bad about themselves. This, of course, can lead to defensiveness, which is exactly what this card is meant to fend off. This flash card takes the sting out of someone being upset with you. It says: "I don't *want to* be upset with you . . . I want to feel received by you. In fact, I want to feel loved by you." To tell your partner that you are just a heartbeat away from feeling loved is a beautiful opportunity to meet someone more than halfway. And it gives that someone the beautiful opportunity to discover again how transformative is their willingness to just listen.

6.

I have no idea what to do right now except to tell you that I am in a lot of pain, I know you are, too, and I want it to be friendlier between us.

If you really consider it, you will realize that this message is your honest-to-God, bottom-line truth a lot more often than you've let yourself know. A relief, isn't it?

Not only is there no shame in having no idea what to do in an unhappy relationship scenario, there is a profound humility and nobility in not pretending otherwise. Do you think there would be so many wars and divorces and general misery on the planet—let alone a book like this one—if anyone really had any Ultimate Idea about how to keep it friendly? So much of our "knowing what to do" is fueled by frantic self-protectiveness: I want to calm you down . . . I want you to feel so guilty, you won't confront me on my stuff . . . I want you to see my good intentions . . . I want to point out all the flaws in your reasoning . . . I want to disappoint you and not have you hate me . . . etc., etc., etc.

I'm sure there are exceptions that prove the rule, but truly, think of any rupture you and your partner have ever had, and think of the most brilliant point or comeback you ever made. At that very moment, might it not also have been true that some other part of you was also clueless and hurting . . . and just wanted things friendlier between you?

This flash card comes to your partner free of any pretense. It is a true white flag. And your willingness to model a "solution-deficient" desire for something kinder between the two of you will make it safer for your partner to feel she deserves friendliness, when she, too, is in pain and out of ideas. So while there may not be an Ultimate Idea of how to keep things friendly between humans, this would usually be a step in the right direction.

7.

I know you want to
repair this, but right now
I just need to be in my
own space. Please—
try not to take this
personally. I love you.

This flash card is a classic example of someone saying "yes" to herself, not "no" to you—but for the person who is geared to actively repairing whatever unpleasantness is currently lying between you—and now!—it may be a drop hard to hear. The purpose of this flash card is to keep their frustration at the level of "a drop"—and ideally dissipate it altogether.

Following a particularly painful exchange between two people, there are many good reasons why one of you might not yet be ready to be in an overtly interactive place with the other person. Perhaps you are still feeling too mad, disappointed or confused (see flash card #8) to believe you can start processing this rupture without making matters worse. You will know this because your mind is still getting happily stimulated pleading your case—not particularly wanting to "repair" anything. Or perhaps you may just be somewhere on the continuum of tired/exhausted/depleted and even a well-meaning call to repair feels like too great a demand on your energy.

But here's the thing with this flash card: it is a sophisticated form of repair unto itself. The Sender is kindly entering the inner world of the person gung ho on reconnecting, by acknowledging both her desire to mend things and the fact that his reluctance will likely make her feel that he's not taking the relationship seriously enough. A few pages back we said a "Please don't take this personally" flash card would be a wasted card. But acknowledging that another *is likely taking it personally* is anything but wasted. Note that the "I love you" isn't just thrown in for filler. It further helps your partner make the sometimes difficult distinction between abandonment and healthy space-taking.

8.

I'm frankly confused about what's going on between us, and need a little time to sort this out. Is that okay with you?

You will notice throughout this manual a number of instances where two or three flash cards seem to say sort of the same thing. Like this one and #7 before it: *"I know you want to repair this, but right now I just need to be in my own space. Please—try not to take this personally. I love you."* This is because the messages carry somewhat different energies, and the more energetically in sync the Sender can be with both the Receiver and the current emotional atmosphere, the more likely the offering of the flash card will be experienced as a loving act.

The previous card is sent with a heightened awareness that the Receiver has a strong, possibly anxiety-driven, need to resolve the disagreement *right now*. With this flash card, the Sender is . . . frankly, confused . . . and his own vulnerability in that acknowledgment is the healing component in the message. The *"Is that okay with you?"* lets his partner know that he is not oblivious to the fact that she might have some feelings about his need

for a little time. And if you think about it, asking for "space" has potentially more of a feel of leaving someone than a request for mere "time."

Relationship upsets are frequently confusing. At any moment our inner kindergartner or eleven-year-old can arrive unannounced, feeling unimportant, bossed or ridiculed. Furthermore, what triggered me ten minutes ago may have had more to do with the time four months ago when you hung up the phone on me than with your just rushing out the door to the airport . . . but how would I know?

Typically in several couples sessions a month I will stop the action and sincerely say to both parties, "Hold it . . . I'm confused." I have never once had a partner indicate in the slightest to me that they were confused as to why I'd be confused. We all know it is pretty confusing.

9.

I don't need you to see
this exactly as I do. But I
do need you to hear
where I am coming from.

There are two good situations in which to use this flash card. The first is when you sense your partner isn't hearing you because they're afraid if they do, they'll have to believe something or do something that is aversive to them. They're afraid that if they really take you seriously, they will have to give up something cherished.

She can't hear why you would want to spend Thanksgiving at a spiritual retreat because it is intolerable and bizarre to her that you would even consider not spending such an important holiday with family at her sister's. He can't hear how unhappy you are with his travel schedule because he's afraid if he does, he will have to modify an important part of his business life. Both parties are at an impasse. What this card does is activate an important principle and that is: you can usually get more "give" from your partner when they can first feel the legitimacy of your predicament than when you are hitting them over the head with it in order to get them to change. We cannot say it enough. You deserve to be heard. But the more you are truly attempting to be heard versus trying to change another person, the more likely they'll bend a little.

The second situation is when you are ready to own up to the fact that *everything you have been doing thus far* has been an effort to get your partner to see things exactly as you do. Welcome to the Human Condition . . . we all have this tendency. The great irony of this flash card is that by acknowledging that you have, indeed, been vigorously attempting to enroll your partner in your version of reality, you will make it much more likely that your partner will relax enough to actually hear the sanity in your version.

10.

There's something really important I need to say to you, and I would like you to *truly* listen—not react (at least for five minutes, anyway).

The essence of this book isn't about giving people the lines. *It is about optimizing the chance that your lines will be received on the other end.* This particular flash card can make that happen quite directly.

Often you know what you wish you could say to your partner. You've gone over it in your head seventeen times. You imagine how real and clear and grown-up you are going to feel when you just say what is in your heart: "I didn't feel great listening to how harsh you sounded helping Brittany with her math homework." "I want to tell you some thoughts I have about our next vacation, and I'm worried you'll be so worried about the cost, you won't even hear out my plan." "I gave you the message yesterday that I really agreed with you that your boss was being insensitive with you. What I didn't tell you was how I also thought you provoked him."

As you get closer to delivering your communication, you notice you are feeling more vague, less sure of yourself, wondering whether you are being too heavy-handed, quite inclined to worry about your partner's defending himself or overexplaining, and whether the ensuing uproar will be worth it. Make it safer for yourself and flash this message. If the Receiver shows a little nervousness, tell them, "Okay, how about just four and a half minutes . . . promise."

If the Receiver responds poorly (*"Now what?"*), simply say, "Your 'now what?' tells me you are expecting something bad to happen . . . This is why I am using this card." This card is a five-minute mute button—a real rarity. Because staying mute will likely be a stretch for her partner, the Sender would do well to speak thoughtfully and noncritically to her silenced combatant should she ever wish to use this flash card successfully a second time.

II.

Fear not . . . I'm not on a tear. I just want to say one simple thing.

If you have been on a tear, good for you that you can actually see this and make the choice to leave the warpath—but that doesn't mean your partner would have any reason to trust that he wasn't about to get an earful.

This flash card should be thought of as sacred. You are telling your wary and potentially overloaded partner that he is safe. We beg you—think twice before flashing this card. Are you really intending to say just one simple thing? Because if your partner is trusting that you mean what the flash card says, and you overstep the bounds, you will do serious damage to the trust between you, and you might as well throw this book out, in terms of future use.

What does one simple thing look like? Glad you asked. Most of us never had a model of what that looks like. So, a few examples: "It hurt that you implied something inappropriate was going on because I had coffee with my old college boyfriend." Period. Or, "I want to be able to tell you that it made me nervous that you were having coffee with an old boyfriend, without you feeling that I am accusing you of adultery." Period. After your partner gets over the shock that you actually have limited yourself to one coherent thought, you may be delighted to find that your simplifying things did, in fact, create an opportunity for closer contact with him or her.

It may have been unfair at the beginning of this field note to assume that you were no stranger to tears. Such a thought precludes the not rare possibility that your partner can be a bit defensive at times and assume you are about to confront her even when you just want to tell her that you're running low on fabric softener or Caesar salad dressing. This card can help at these times as well—particularly if you don't treat such occurrences as emergencies.

12.

I've been so focused on being heard, I didn't see how much sense you are really making.

This flash card is a dream come true for many reasons—not the least of which is that the Sender is owning how his own self-absorption interfered with his ability to truly see and hear you. Offered unbidden, this not flashy flash card is worth about a year of good psychotherapy.

It requires real humility to offer this message, and this is one of those cases where you might first need to imagine how good it would make you feel to be given this flash card, to then inspire you to want to offer it.

Notice, by the way, that we are talking here about your partner's point of view "making sense"—not that she is necessarily "right." When I am focused on my own need to be heard, I am unable to enter your frame of reference. And only when we are able to enter each other's worlds can we come to a decision that is organically right.

I remember an engaged couple in major gridlock because one of them, a New Age nurse obsessed with autism and compromised immune systems, couldn't imagine vaccinating her yet unconceived child. Her mainstream lawyer fiancé had never heard of such a radical view and thought it insane not to vaccinate a newborn. Each was vehemently arguing their position until I required them to fully take on the other's perspective. Out of nowhere, the future mother, who had been the more vociferous of the two, declared, "I can see how frightening it would be to Barry to not give his child something that 98 percent of the pediatricians in America would deem necessary." That she stopped there—and no longer needed to push her view that these pediatricians were misguided—showed her love of Barry. And when he made sense to her, he felt loved.

13.

I was making a big deal
out of something that
just isn't that important.
I want to let it go.

As the power of the flash card lies in the spirit of authenticity in which it is offered, it is important that this message be used because you really see you have blown something out of proportion—not because you just want peace. Not that peace is a bad thing but because if you really have something bothering you that ought to be resolved, "letting it go" sounds good on paper, but you can rest assured that it will come back later to haunt you.

That being said, my God! . . . How many times have you gotten annoyed by something—often something small—and the thing took on a life of its own? You've told your wife how important it is to you to have soy milk in the house at all times. You cannot eat your cereal without it, and you have cereal every morning. The world knows this. And now . . . no soy milk in the house. And you are, as they say, "carrying on." You're worried about whether your husband is spending enough time with your six-month-old daughter. You know the fact that your father walked out on your mother when you were an infant plays into this, but it is almost intolerable to you when you see your husband make what looks like perfunctory contact with your child. And now he's playing his guitar and little Ashley's in an infant carrier on the floor, and for several minutes, he doesn't seem to be looking at her. And you are, as they say, "carrying on."

Wanting your partner to be mindful of your special needs is perfectly legitimate. And who would argue with wanting your husband to have a real and loving relationship with his child? But there comes a moment when it hits you that some old button inside you has been pushed . . . And you realize how exhausted your wife is. And you remember how yesterday your husband was making goo-goo eyes with Ashley while guitar-playing. There really is no danger. You can truly let it go without losing anything—while gaining a lot. Like peace.

PART II

Setting
Limits

Think of this set of flash cards as interpersonal stop signs. They are to be used when the energy between you and your partner is anywhere from heartbreakingly frustrating to rageful. These are for those times when it feels like something is spiraling out of control and you are feeling overwhelmed by your partner and/or your own inability to do anything that wouldn't just throw fuel on the fire. While the last set of cards was more or less gentle in encouraging a changing of gears, this set indicates loud and clear that you want to stop the direction your interaction is going in—now.

Simple sanity is often the perfect antidote to insanity. These flash cards can work with the very angry and/or the very crazed beloved in your life because they offer a loud and clear "No" to what feels like craziness, rather than doing what we usually do in the face of relentlessness or unreasonableness—either relentlessly and unreasonably resist them or freeze.

Because these messages are often employed when one's nervous system is in high-gear fight-or-flight, they actually can have the most dramatic impact in reversing the direction of an unhappy encounter. This is because the kindness inherent in the act of intelligently choosing to offer a flash card has been documented to quickly alter the body chemistry of hyper-aroused combatants who have been in a state where self-soothing is all but impossible. The flash card becomes an agent of external soothing, telegraphing to the Receiver the most important message of all: *You are safe*.

Interestingly, though I gave it some thought, there seemed no reason to include a flash card in this book "You are safe" or even a better one that said, "I want you to feel safer with me." This is because assurances are almost completely useless when you are feeling endangered. But a partner demonstrating goodwill and some straightforward vulnerability—say, calmly communicating to the relentless person in front of him that she is being a bully right now—can contribute enormously to the safety in the room.

14.

I'm feeling very scared
of you right now.

When you are feeling threatened by someone it is admittedly asking a lot to expect you to remember that only someone who was feeling frightened themselves would need to act so scary. But it's a truth of human nature that we often become loud, intransigent and threatening when we feel "little" to someone else's "big." This powerful flash card can act like a wonder drug with your seemingly unreachable partner by instantly transforming you in front of their eyes into someone littler and therefore less intimidating. Offering the statement on this card can literally level the psychological playing field. It catapults the scared person, quietly and valiantly flashing this card, into much more of an equal. And if you think about it, people who aren't feeling inferior or superior to each other are rarely particularly antagonistic.

By the way, this card isn't for just when your partner is yelling, belligerent or otherwise overtly acting out. You can be quite scared of someone who is sullen or uncommunicative. You can also be quite scared of someone who is speaking calmly but is just not making a whole lot of sense. Regardless of their particular form of frightening, this card will instantly calm the Receiver and "mature" them, so they move from scaring you to providing you with the love you need.

15.

I am your friend. It's painful seeing how quickly I can become your enemy.

have personally witnessed or heard reports of literally hundreds upon hundreds of scenarios in which loving, intimate partners have polarized in a nanosecond. And I'm not talking here about the instant you discover that your husband has actually been conducting a complex love life on an interactive porn site. I'm talking about little stuff, or what you'd think would be little stuff. Let's take driving routes as an extremely common example.

Ben and Sue are driving from their home in the suburbs to see a movie downtown. They truly start out in a terrific, happy mood, really liking each other. Ben is driving and automatically takes the local back-roads route he takes to work every day.

"What are you doing? Take the expressway!" gasps Sue, as if endangered. *"We'll never make the movie if you go that way!"* Should Ben not heed Sue's warning, and fast, she may well become frantic—a combination of her fear of being late and her belief that her invaluable advice is not being taken seriously. As Sue continues in emergency mode, this would be a time for Ben to use this flash card.

But there are other ways this driving thing can go. Ben is driving again, and calmly, Sue offers, "Do you think it might be wiser to get onto 76? It might be the speedier way to head out this time of day." That's all she says, but Ben immediately flips out. *"For crying out loud, will you quit bugging me! Don't you think I can think for myself? What's with you . . . are you trying to start a fight?"* etc., etc., etc. This would be a time for Sue to use this flash card.

I cannot tell you how common both scenarios are. Likely, if you keep a copy of this book in the car, it will get as much use as if kept anywhere else. It has been suggested to this author that she make some sort of arrangement with Toyota or General Motors for all new cars to come with a set of Flash Cards for Real Life in the glove compartment.

Being in a car with your partner creates

forced proximity, and when you each have a different picture of the ideal route, you have an instant differentiation crisis: *My partner isn't me*. Such conditions, in a car or out, can quickly turn a friend into an adversary. Allow this flash card to remind your partner of your friendship.

16.

When you go on and on like that, I feel invisible to you.

In the universe of all possibilities, this is one of the most therapeutic responses you can give yourself and your partner when they are relentlessly talking at you, not to you. In my experience, it's a rare person who didn't grow up being talked *at*, fairly regularly, by at least one parent. As a consequence, for many of us there is a lingering sense of not feeling visible to the people who matter most to us. We can't quite say our parents didn't love us . . . but it's hard *to have felt loved* if you didn't feel seen.

So when your partner is going on and on at you and you flash this message, you are giving both your inner child and your outer adult the gift of showing up free of the self-judgment and self-depreciation you internalized at a much younger age. You are finally having a moment of being invalidated or stampeded or simply lectured to by a significant other *without interpreting it* as you being unimportant, stupid, uninteresting, not compelling enough, unworthy or just plain bad. Labeling your experience as "feeling invisible" hits the nail on the head and brings you into Reality, where you are finally noticing you are at the mercy of a blind person. This is a revelation that can allow you to stop doing to yourself what you have been doing for decades—*thinking there is something wrong with you because you can't get a blind person to see.* Which is why we think this card is so therapeutic . . . and not just for you.

First of all, you've brought the Receiver's self-absorption to their attention. You haven't shamed them for any particular thought or perspective they might have. You are simply asking them to notice all the space they take up, and how little is left for you.

Gratifying, isn't it, to imagine that in less than a minute, without fanfare, you can get your favorite person to transcend their self-absorption and truly recognize their impact on you?

17.

Rather than just criticize me, can you tell me what you want in a more positive way?

I am not entirely certain why, but the fact is that most of us are embedded in criticism as a way of life. How will Monica get Richard to see how unimportant and taken for granted she feels if she doesn't tell him how insensitive he is when he arrives home twenty-five minutes late without having called? How will she absolutely make sure he doesn't do it again if she doesn't ensure he feels terrible and really gets this as evidence of a serious character flaw? How will Richard get Monica to make more home-cooked meals if he doesn't imply that all the takeout they've been having recently is evidence of fiscal irresponsibility and—though he's smart enough to imply it without using the exact word—laziness?

This flash card is more radical than meets the eye. Think how rare this is: the Sender isn't ignoring his critic or defending himself or even invalidating her criticisms. He is telling her he'd rather not be criticized but that still isn't stopping him from wanting to give her what she wants. Only she has to make her wants more important than making him feel bad. *Can she do this*? She will be disarmed, trust me. It won't come naturally. She will have to think about it before consciously choosing to let go of her critical stance.

But imagine what it would do for your relationship if every time one of you would normally reach for criticism, you began, instead, with, "I'd feel so loved if you . . ."

18.

I hate feeling that I have to walk on eggshells around you.

If I had to name one thing that in my experience makes couples the most uncomfortable most of the time, hands down it would be when one or both parties feels they have to walk on eggshells around their partner. To be so worried about someone's reaction that you either cannot open your mouth or have to so make nice that you might as well not have spoken . . . is a kind of agony.

When you are so aware of your partner's unspoken hair-trigger reactivity that anything you might want to share pales in comparison with the seemingly life-and-death requirement to prevent any discomfort that might cause them to snap out and—as often is the case—self-righteously explode and/or shut down any further communication, believe me when I say you have no other choice than to let your partner know, if even just for your own sanity. There's an interesting phrase relevant to this: "99 percent a bitch, 100 percent an angel." What it means is that when I am walking on eggshells around you—holding back even 1 percent—ironically, it comes across with an edge. There's a jaggedness that comes with my inauthenticity with you, stemming from having to manage your feelings rather than stay with my own. But when I can tell you how it *really* is for me . . . when I'm so free with you that I am without filters . . . when I can just relax into being myself . . . I move to the angelic realm. Use this card if any of the above fits your situation and I can virtually promise you, you will create safety where you didn't think it possible.

19.

You are being a bully.

This card seemingly breaks all the rules of conscious communication. It's no "I statement," it's making an accusation, it's not showing much vulnerability and, in some circles, it would be considered name-calling. So why is it that, in almost all the cases I've heard about, the Receiver reported feeling kind of loved when his partner held this message up to him?

Well, try it on yourself. Imagine sternly giving your partner an ultimatum like, "I will cancel our reservations to Aruba unless you _____ (e.g., get rid of the clutter in the den, make sure every last one of those kittens is adopted, agree to see a sex therapist . . . or any one of a million highly desired preferences on your part)." And after a little vigorous bickering on the point, your partner leaves the room and returns flashing this flash card. It feels kind of like a kiss, doesn't it— particularly when you think of all the other ways they could have reacted to you?

This card works so well because, used appropriately, it tells the truth, but without giving your partner a taste of their own medicine. The Receiver instantly feels the disparity between their own rigidity and the gentleness being extended to them . . . and you will likely feel mildly shamed but really, mostly grateful that you have such a kind partner. This card is a real demonstration of the gold inherent in conscious communication in general, and these flash cards, in particular. The Receiver feels loved because, despite the fact that they have had a tyrannical moment, you not only are refusing to clobber them back, but are staying in a friendly relationship with them.

Feeling into this possibility, it may be hard to wait for the next time your partner starts bullying you, just so you can have the pleasure of staying sane in their presence.

20.

Talk to me like I'm someone you love.

This was the message that inspired this book, and almost twenty years after first scribbling it on a scrap of paper for a beleaguered husband in my office, I am still touched by something uncompromisingly self-loving—something so pristine—in this declaration.

I encourage all readers to experiment with this flash card, if only to give yourself a really good taste of what true centeredness feels like. The ostensibly simple request, "Talk to me like I'm someone you love," can infuse the most mean-spirited interactions with new levels of respect and self-respect. I have heard story after story of individuals locked in combative gridlock with partners who, with Gandhi-like dignity, have penetrated steel walls by ignoring all manner of criticism and attack, and doing nothing else but holding up this flash card.

Many of us grew up with parents who loved us but who didn't talk to us like they did. If, by some miracle, as children we had been in touch enough with ourselves to confront a difficult parent with this message, we would have at once been connected to our pain, to our self-worth *and* to our parent. So, from the childhood wounding perspective, this phrase is a deeply empowering and relational one. But it is also powerful because it radically ignores the content of whatever is bothering the person to whom you want to say this, and quickly gets to the heart of the matter: in this thing we call a relationship, how *are* we going to treat each other?

There are very few bad things you or your partner could do that would ever have more valence than your belief that both of you deserve to be treated lovingly, despite it all.

21.

Right now, I don't need a lecture. I need your love.

While the previous flash card has the tone of quiet dignity (think Gandhi), #21 is a little snappier. While it ostensibly asks the Receiver to stop with the scolding, it is actually asking for something much, much bigger—for your partner to get out of their head and into their heart.

We get very wedded to our lectures . . . very. But hearing our beloved suggest baldly, "I need your love more than your lecture" is such a grand invitation that we might actually be willing to see that our lecture, no matter how well-intentioned, isn't the highest expression of our love. To the part of your partner that has equated love with saving your soul, this flash card could initially leave you disoriented on very new ground.

For all of you out there whose partners are psychotherapists—real professional ones or junior ones who make psychoanalyzing you their hobby—you can really shake things up if you doctor the card (to use a phrase) and rewrite it: *"Right now I don't need a shrink. I need your love."*

I can speak personally as the occasional recipient of this one. It can come as a jolt to the part of you that has been under the delusion that the Shrink in you and the Lover are one and the same.

22.

I know you're feeling nagged, but please stay . . . When you walk away from me, I feel discarded.

Not to be sexist or anything but I have heard far more reports of men walking out of rooms with women following them than vice versa. For those of you reading this who are thinking, "Not in my house, sister . . . !" I totally believe you—just adjust what I am about to say accordingly.

I'm using this flash card as an opportunity to tell you about some compelling research that has trickled down from infant studies into couples therapy. Drawing on the neurobiological roots of connection, Drs. Patricia Love and Steven Stosny report in *How to Improve Your Marriage Without Having to Talk About It* (Broadway Books, 2007) that infant girls are hardwired to respond to attachment disruption (i.e., emotional and/or physical withdrawal) with fear, while boys—even less than two months old—automatically respond to a mother's abrupt departure with shame.

The authors make a convincing case that however reasonably it is presented, a woman's "Honey, we have to talk" can trigger feelings of inadequacy in men. In other words, your guy is not hearing your persistence as a bid for closeness, but more as something akin to an invitation to the vice principal's office— and he'll do anything to escape his feelings of shame. In the typical (and, admittedly, stereotypical) scenario, his distancing co-creates nagging. And her relentlessness only works to reinforce his feeling that he is on the verge of being humiliated.

The beauty of this flash card is that its Sender is acknowledging what the Receiver is going through *and* taking an important chunk of responsibility for it by acknowledging that she is being a bit of a nag. But she (or he) also is sending the message loud and clear that (remember what I said about psychological stop signs?) his exiting from the interaction midstream is causing her (or him!) to feel kind of thrown away. We don't want him to feel more shame, but we do want him to see what his impact on her has been.

Please use common sense here, ladies. When the card gets him to stay, don't just see it as an opportunity to resume nagging.

23.

What you are saying is worth listening to, but I am so totally flooded, I can't take in one more thing. I wish I could, but I can't.

The "flooding" here refers to the physiological arousal that occurs in an intense upset with a partner and our pulse is rapid, our blood pressure is skyrocketing, we are flushing, sweating, tensing our muscles and breathing more rapidly. According to John Gottman, Ph.D., arguably the world's most astute researcher of marital interaction, the flooding process begins for the average man or woman when his/her resting pulse increases by 10 percent. If, for either sex, the heart rate goes to one hundred beats per minute, adrenaline starts secreting sufficiently that a fight-or-flight response is triggered, leaving one feeling like they are fighting for their life. However, in most cases, the guy's blood pressure and heart rate will rise much higher than a woman's and stay that way. And it takes far less conflict for a man to become physiologically overwhelmed than his female counterpart. And as we've already learned, her arousal makes her want to engage more—to keep the contact going whether it is "pleasant" or not. Someone who is using this flash card is trying to tell you that what is going on right now is not only unpleasant—it is intolerable.

If you, who tends to become flooded relatively easily, make the momentous decision to use this flash card, you are a true Prince (or Princess), as you are doing the near-impossible—demonstrating the humanity to remember that you live in a relational field with a vulnerable person capable of feeling abandoned and/or discarded by you—while your body is telling you to think about no one but yourself.

The person receiving this flash card is now faced with a corresponding challenge: to note that a part of them is absolutely *feeling* abandoned by a loved one seemingly leaving the field, and at the same time to make the choice—for it is a choice—to see their partner's enormous decency and heart in flashing this message before taking cover.

24.

All I'm feeling right now is your "position." I need you to come back so I can relate to you— not your position.

Two years into their marriage, Maggie, a New Age massage therapist, was aghast to discover that Harry, her supposedly liberal husband—he campaigned for Obama, is anti all wars, and on top of that is a meticulous recycler—actually longed to enact a family tradition of flying the American flag on the Fourth of July. Admittedly, Harry had kept this from her, anticipating it would offend her more bohemian sensibilities—and, in fairness to Maggie, his concealment of this for over four years of their relationship, though possibly comprehensible, was not ideal. She shrieked:

"An American flag? On my lawn? My clients are going to see an American flag on my lawn? Are you out of your friggin' mind? Am I going to find out next that you belong to the NRA? How dare you keep this from me? Can't you think for yourself? Who cares if it is a 'family tradition'? Suppose your family supported lynching . . ."

This anecdote, by the way, was reported the following day by Maggie, a client of mine.

When threatened, we often think that if we don't defend our position we're not being true to ourselves, and in the moment, Maggie might have said she was letting "the real Maggie" hang out. Little could be further from the truth. Our positions turn our loved ones into enemies, not confidants.

Had he successfully used this flash card, Harry might have accessed what took his wife two therapy sessions to figure out. The "You" who was missing in her initial outburst would have told her husband that she associates people who have the accoutrements of patriotism with people who give their power away to Authority, people who don't think for themselves—people like her father, who once believed a nun in junior high school who thought Maggie had instigated a prank, rather than listening to Maggie, who told him she was innocent. And, as it frequently goes, Maggie had married a man who gave his authority away *to her* by not sharing an uncomfortable difference between them.

25.

I'm already feeling awful. Do you really think I haven't heard you?

In compiling what I hope to be a serious relationship repair manual, I have aimed to keep glib and smart-ass energy out of these flash cards entirely. However, this is one flash card that might be veering toward the mildly exasperated. My only defense is that it feels a notch realer and friendlier than a flash card that says, "Enough, already!" Then again, maybe not. My hope is that the Sender, who likely has done something that did legitimately bug her partner, is conveying that she's not trying to wiggle out of something—she truly feels bad—but at the same time . . . "Enough, already!"

Much has been said about the need to express oneself authentically. This whole book is about sharing yourself this way. But another aspect of communication is noting whether your communication is actually being taken in and thoughtfully digested by your partner. Often we are so wounded in this area, and our expectations are so low, that we go on and on as if we still haven't gotten through . . . when we actually have.

I like this flash card. It lets the Receiver know he has made his point, you feel appropriate remorse . . . and there are still *two* human beings in this interaction. It is rare that someone who is flashed this card then says, "No, I don't think you are really hearing me." The Receiver now feels a tad bad—maybe not awful, but chastened—realizing he has overdone it. The Sender is demonstrating her goodwill be offering this flash card, even if it is a bit sardonic. That's because she hasn't left the field in exasperation, and is now pinpointing the most current relationship issue between them—that he doesn't fully trust that she's receiving him.

And in the long run, it's probably a better issue to look at between them than the initial grievance she was feeling awful about. As always with couples, how you relate to the issue *is* the issue.

26.

I want us to stop what we are doing to each other. Both of us. Now . . .

Good for you, knowing that it is both of you . . . even if a part of you doesn't really believe it, and you can present a pretty good case about how mature and flow-y this relationship would be if your partner weren't so petty, thin-skinned, obsessive, narrow-minded, cruel or unwilling to explore his relationship with his mother.

Your partner may be all of those things and more, but you are the one who is reacting to him, and it's getting pretty unattractive. In fact, if you are honest with yourself, when you are confronting him about where he is just so off, you are sounding pretty much the way you sounded when you were fourteen and battling your mother in the dressing room at Lord & Taylor. (Sorry to be the messenger here . . .)

No one would think of sending this flash card if they weren't in a pretty exhausted and unhappy state, when it really is the most natural thing in the world to see what your partner is doing to you—how unreasonable he is being. The fact that the Sender is not coming from a victim position—that she is making it mutual . . . that the "Now" is speaking to some backbone in her that gets the two of you are not handling things in the way she knows you are capable of at your best—makes this a very compelling message.

". . . what we are doing to each other. Both of us." This is a willingness to honor your partnership when it would be so easy to blame, to take sides, as it were. Imagine your "adversary" holding up this message to you. There's a sweetness to it. And there's something comforting about finding out there's still a grown-up in the room.

PART III

Feeling Vulnerable

When someone begins therapy with me, I rarely begin by taking a full history. Instead, I simply ask the client to imagine being in fifth grade and befriending a kid in their class whom they really like. And then finding out that the new chum is having a birthday party to which they would have presumed to be invited—only they weren't. Most people will say they'd feel hurt. Then I ask them two questions: Would you have told your mom how you felt? (A significant minority would not.) And if you told her, how would she have responded?

Invariably, the answers fall into a few categories: the "rational" mom who tells you that there will be other parties and/or that she never liked that kid anyway; the "protective" mom who gets activated, if not outraged, and calls the kid's mother and lobbies for an invitation; the "depleted or depressed" mom who has little energy to even hear what is going on; the "detective" mom who pointedly investigates why you failed to earn an invitation; and the "nurturing" mom who tells you how wonderful you are and promises to take you to the movies the day of the party.

I go down this road because I want to know one important thing—how your early universe related to you when you were vulnerable. I cannot tell you how rare it is that someone reports a parent who simply recognized their vulnerability and joined them there: "That must really hurt, Billy. I know how much you love playing with Howie, and how left out you must be feeling. I'm so sorry you have to deal with this. I remember when Cheryl Sapperstein didn't invite me to her sweet sixteen party, and how miserable I felt."

A couple of extra-credit questions you can ask yourself with regard to how your vulnerability was received (or not received) as a child: How would your mother have responded if you specifically told her that you felt left out? And, how would your father have responded if you expressed the same feelings to him? There's no one to blame here—particularly if you imagine what it would have been like for your parents to have attempted to be vulnerable with their own parents. As I've said before, when it comes to conscious communication, we're still in the prehistoric age.

Why does all this matter? Because intimacy cannot happen if we are not in more or less comfortable relationship with our own insides in the company of our partner. As long as I stay in the self-protective mode I adapted to in my family of origin, I will never really feel close to you or make it safe for you to feel close to me. Stark but true.

So, vulnerability-wise, it's hard enough to know that the offhand sarcastic remark you made in response to discovering that your partner had had a long and enthusiastic chat with her college roommate that day is really covering up feeling "left out." Harder still to be anything other than reactive when your partner innocently misses the point that you feel this way. It can feel almost impossible to do anything other than just react, defend yourself or otherwise contract when you're in a majorly adversarial or otherwise unsafe place with someone you are close to. For most of us, the instinctive response is to try to manage the *perceived* loss of connection or sense of feeling diminished by being defensive. Typically, defensiveness is what arises when I am feeling unseen or devalued, or when I'm worried that either one of us is thinking less of me.

The flash cards in this section are specifically designed to help you loosen the grip when your instinct is to protect yourself from feeling insignificant, weak, needy, awkward, not with it, unlovable and all the other states of being we were taught are icky, rather than beautifully human, which is what they are.

When you told your mom how bad you felt that you didn't get invited to that fifth-grade party, the obvious place of vulnerability, where she might not have been able to meet you, was around feeling rejected by a desirable playmate. Less obvious was that no one recognized how much that kid mattered to you . . . that you *cared*. And even less obvious, but maybe most relevant to the current state of your relationship life, was no one recognizing your vulnerability in bringing your heartache to your mom in the first place. She likely missed that her getting it—no, her getting *you*—mattered so much to you. And so now, a part of you isn't even sure that wanting someone to see your vulnerability is an okay thing to want.

I am here to tell you that wanting someone, particularly a special someone, to recognize your vulnerability is wanting that person to see the real you. And this is a very good thing to want.

27.

When you talk to me
that way, I just feel small.

Though you may have to think about this for a moment, this flash card has enormous shock value. This is because if your partner is like many people, she or he has no idea how they come across when they: point out how you totally blew a wonderful opportunity to bond with your stepson last night . . . wonder why you bought a can of crushed tomatoes with basil when you were instructed to buy a can of unseasoned whole tomatoes . . . applaud a neighbor's willingness to spend a weekend at a sexual enrichment workshop that they know you think is slightly kooky . . . or analyze an unpleasant interaction you had with your boss in terms of what never got resolved between you and your high school tennis coach.

It is likely your partner is feeling that they are being truly helpful in pointing out these truths. And, in some small or not small way, they are operating under the unquestioned belief that "you really need to get this."

Part of why you are feeling small is because your partner is probably right, or at least somewhat right about something, but, frankly, this small feeling should only be a momentary pinprick in time. And it would be . . . if your partner could simply acknowledge that what they are saying is making you feel vulnerable. They aren't consciously trying to put you down—they are just so enthralled with their own agenda and so lacking in delicacy that they don't see you and how their agenda is making you feel. This flash card can stop them dead in their tracks when they are going down this road. It will also help you become more comfortable with the idea that it doesn't matter so much that you screwed up or disappointed someone. *What matters is that you found the courage to tell them how you felt about how they told you.* Counterintuitive, I know . . . but try it.

"Small" is how I feel when my imperfections seem to make you forget how big I really am.

28.

I know I sounded extremely angry, but I was feeling more threatened than you could possibly have known.

A compassionate way of looking at a rageaholic is not as someone who frequently blows up—or, as typically is the case, frequently gets "reactive"—but as someone who does not give themselves permission to own their own vulnerability and needs. Such a person might angrily express being "snubbed" when an acquaintance doesn't respond to a casual e-mail, rather than allow herself to simply feel that it hurts or makes her feel unimportant. It is extremely scary for some people to acknowledge that other people's affection or consideration matters to them. Take road rage as a case in point. I truly believe that it's not that the offending driver almost killed us that bothers us—it's that their whizzing by us or not moving fast enough is treating us as if we don't exist. This is what fuels rage.

While most people I know are not what I'd call rageaholics or road ragers, there aren't too many I'd call consistently peaceful either.

All of them have the potential to become "easily irritated." I began this piece writing about rageaholics in order to depict what we *all* tend to do when threatened: mask our fear of loss or sense of being diminished with victim-y anger and unchecked testiness.

Use this flash card when the rageaholic in you has come out. You screamed your little head off because your partner failed to do something that mattered to you, and this morphed into a bitter documenting of every failure of theirs you can recall. Your partner now won't talk to you or respond to your most desperate apologies. This flash card will remind even a psychologically unaware partner of how threatened you had to have been to behave like that. Then it's your job to tell your partner how your own preexisting wiring and wounding caused their infraction to make you feel more insignificant than they'd have any reason to know.

29.

I'm afraid to be
real with you.

This flash card could easily have gone in a number of fancier directions: "I'm afraid if I'm real with you, you'll be mad at me . . . you won't like me . . . you'll feel criticized instead of seeing what I'm struggling with . . . you'll see me as mean . . . you'll take it personally . . . you won't value my realness . . . you'll want to leave me . . . you won't understand why I need to be real with you . . . I'll find out you prefer me being unreal." And so on.

It's fair to say this flash card encompasses all of the above, with probably the last worry—"I'll find out you prefer me being unreal"—being the scariest, in that it confirms one of our worst fears: that our partner is not big enough to support us in being true to ourselves. Which then leads to even more trouble when we come to the conclusion that a part of us will have to hate this person or wonder what the hell we are doing with them. Which is why this ostensibly simple flash card requires a lot of courage to flash. *A lot* is on the line.

There are times in a relationship when you realize that what you've told yourself is being diplomatic or non-confrontational is actually humoring your partner . . . and the falseness is eating away at you. Blake needed to tell his partner, Andrew, that his superior attitude with his younger brother was diminishing his respect for him. Sharon needed to tell Walt that his drinking was driving her away, and that he was an alcoholic who needed help. Ryan needed to tell his wife, Patricia, that even though she was an incest survivor, it was no longer okay with him to go months and months without sexual contact. Molly needed to tell her husband, Richard, that he just plain talked too much last night when they went out to dinner with another couple and that she was embarrassed.

But don't tell your partner that thing you couldn't tell him or her yet. Don't deprive yourself of the compelling breakthrough conversation that could catapult your relationship into a whole new galaxy.

Telling your partner—from a place of self-responsibility, not blame—how frightening it's been for you, across the board, to be real with them will peel away layer upon layer of tension you have been living with. And trust me, your capacity to make nice predates ever meeting your partner.

30

When you won't communicate with me, I feel like I'm nothing to you.

In the classic scenario, the male who wants to escape because his partner is overwhelming him doesn't take the time to shoot off a friendly and relational explanatory flash card before cutting off contact with his offending sweetie. He typically engages in what researcher John Gottman calls "stonewalling," i.e., maintaining a "stone face," speaking very little or not at all, and sometimes intensified by crossed arms and exasperated eye-rolling—telegraphing quite clearly "Stay away!" Women are known to react quite poorly to this stance, and they tend to get more intense, if not frantic, in an attempt to break through and reestablish contact.

Gottman, who has been observing couples microscopically for more than twenty-five years, reports that the most important variable in long-term relationship happiness is that the woman truly feels she has some power to influence her man. Some of this is because of how indoctrinated most women are into a culture of male dominance. So when her partner refuses to even *hear* her perspective, any subterranean feelings of unfairness start arising pronto. To use an analogy that comes from relationship master Harville Hendrix, Ph.D., the hailstorm confronts the turtle.

Only hailstorms, you may have noticed, have poor track records getting turtles to leave their shells. The only way to break the stalemate here is for the Hailstorm to bravely acknowledge that she, too, has been in a sort of a shell, albeit a noisy one, using nagging and protest in order to camouflage how powerless and unimportant she really feels around you.

Note that this flash card is not a call to be heard more or taken more seriously. At this point, you are asking your tentative partner only to appreciate his impact on you. After flashing this card, you may feel so felt that you could have less of a need to communicate, literally, for days.

31.

I'm embarrassed to say that I don't even remember what I'm arguing with you about.

Watching the many hundreds of couples I've counseled argue, and having gotten in a few of my own extended marital arguments, I can tell you that it is not at all uncommon to find yourself in a combative situation where you have truly lost the ground you started on.

This is how it can happen. Marla was upset because Larry bought her some items from Victoria's Secret that were a bit more risqué than she would have bought for herself—nothing that outlandish, she admitted, but for her, "a stretch." "This feels like asking me to prostitute myself," Marla told her husband, and then reminded him of the time seven years ago when he brought home an X-rated movie without asking her first. Larry then dealt with his shame and exasperation by launching into a speech on the total impossibility of buying anything for his wife that she really would like. To which she replied that it's obvious that he doesn't buy gifts for her in the first place—only for himself. They're off and running, with Larry feeling both ashamed and dizzy.

Since Marla and Larry were clients of mine, I can tell you that this would have been a very different scenario if early on Marla had said, "When you buy me underwear like that, it makes me feel like I'm not appealing enough to you as is," and then eventually Larry got to express, "I admit I had some self-interest in choosing those items, but I wouldn't have bought you something that I didn't think there was a pretty good chance you'd also like. It hurts me when you see me as totally lacking in sensitivity." When you and your partner can begin in this mode, it is a wonderful thing. When you have forgotten what's true, this card stops you from spiraling beyond your comprehension, so that you can more quickly get down to the core of things—that both of you want to be seen and to be loved.

32.

It's frightening to me that we see things so differently.

Ken remembers how thrilling it was meeting Lily for the first time. Not only did she share his enthusiasm for backpacking and cycling, she was an "almost vegetarian" like he was, and . . . miracle of miracles, she was also into meditation. Less than eighteen months later, he tells me with a sardonic chuckle how disturbing it was to find out that she was revolted by tofu and not interested in trying out his particular brand of Buddhist meditation.

What gets stickier is when you find out that your beloved holds dear actual values that you consider so "not you." (How easy it is to see the other as "rigid" and oneself as "acting with integrity.") Now, Ken and his fiancée, Lily, are at war over tipping repair people who come to their home. Ken absolutely believes that it's insulting not to tip a repair person, and that it is the only way to ensure high-quality service "the next time." Lily feels that the kind of tips Ken is suggesting are totally unnecessary, if not frivolous.

To have a happy marriage, these two do not have to have a unified tipping policy. But they *do* have to sit with the discomfort of their differences, acknowledge how scary this can be and thoughtfully listen to the other's thoughts and feelings around the wounding and wiring that led them to their respective positions. This flash card helps you both remember that we're not in relationships to convert each other, but to listen.

33.

I'm starting to disappear.
It feels like there's no
space for me.

It's not uncommon with couples for one partner to typically take up a lot more psychic space and for the other to feel less defined and, not unusually, to be less verbal. Frequently, the former felt drowned out as a child by overwhelming parents while the latter learned they would be safe if they learned to be a very good audience. Couples like this can go on this way for a very long time, because what we therapists would call their "trailing edge" needs are being served in such an arrangement.

For those of you who tend to identify with being a good audience for your partner—and may be *too* comfortable with the spotlight anyplace but on you—this is a flash card worth earmarking. You know who I'm talking about. You know all the times you put yourself aside to make your loved one comfortable—to not stress them by *actually requiring them* to hear you out.

Right this minute, imagine saying to your partner, "I'm starting to disappear. It feels like there's no space for me." And notice what it's like to start making yourself feel visible to yourself. Say it to yourself eighty times. Shout it in a crowd. To know that you are starting to disappear is a pretty high level of consciousness, and for reasons that I hope are now apparent, this is one of the few flash cards in this book that I suggest you practice embodying before using. Think of all the times you pretended to listen to your partner. Imagine the next time you could potentially disappear and what it would be like to flash this card instead.

Keep in mind that that partner of yours who takes up all that space just might be this way because they fear that if they don't initiate squatter's rights on your attention span, they, too, might cease to exist. You might want to start talking with them about all of this.

Admittedly, many couples are not this polarized, but the dynamics can apply to all of us when we are called into being a captive audience.

34.

It's hard admitting I might be wrong.

Yes, it is. But acknowledging it will have you feeling virtuous, clean of heart, congruent, peaceful and deeply appreciated by your partner—particularly if you drove him crazy before you saw the light.

There's nothing more to say. You know what to do.

35.

I'm afraid that if I say I'm sorry, you'll make everything all my fault.

You didn't do what you had promised your spouse you were going to do in terms of getting all your tax data together before going to the accountant. It's really delaying everything and now your husband and your accountant are upset with you. But inside of you, something is screaming, "It's not fair!" Who has time for an "extra" task like taxes when nobody helped me with Nathaniel's birthday party or the laundry or picking up *your* aunt Audrey at the airport? So you've been spending the last ten minutes vigorously explaining all you've been doing for the last three weeks, that you are not a sloth and that even in your sleep you make a positive contribution to the betterment of mankind.

Then it dawns on you: I really have to do the taxes, come to think of it; I've known for years the deadline is April 15—and no one has really been making ultra-unreasonable demands on me.

Flash this message, and when your partner takes it in, quietly add, "I know what's my fault—and it's a lot."

This message is particularly useful when your partner has been insensitive ("Do you really need a third brownie?"), but your violent reaction makes their insensitivity pale in comparison. This is for when you know your partner deserves an apology and you notice you are reluctant to give one, fearful their insensitivity toward *you* will get lost in the shuffle.

This message is NOT to be used when you have done something deeply disturbing, and rightfully so, to your partner, such as verbally attacking a child, relapsing in regard to your addiction or flirting provocatively with another. In certain morally questionable situations it is just poor form, weak and insulting to lobby for equitable co-attribution.

36.

Do you hate me?

This flash card is a jewel. I truly believe that if everyone were in touch with this ever-present question percolating inside them, there would be no wars. Take note:

In a pseudo-caring manner, Glenda wondered aloud whether her husband, Greg, might have attention deficit disorder because he forgot to stop at the drugstore to pick up a few requested items. Resenting her approach, Greg snapped back at her, "Why stop with ADD—have you thought about Alzheimer's?" and walked out of the room. Glenda followed him. "It was only a question," she defended herself, and then took the moral high ground, making the issue Greg's thin-skinned-ness and how easily he withdraws from her. The more she lectured on his "inability to hang in there," the stonier he became. While there is much coaching we could give Greg, for now I want to focus on Glenda.

A good hypothesis is that she is projecting her guilt over her aggressiveness when Greg walked in empty-handed onto him. Make no mistake—he *is* upset with her, but the deeper truth is that his upset pales in comparison to the self-hatred she is projecting onto him. As kids, when our parents got upset over small mishaps, we believed we were very bad. So Glenda takes the superior position to protect herself from feeling that her initial negativity over his forgetfulness marks her as horrid.

Oh, Glendas out there—and there are millions of you—it won't be easy, but give yourself the gift of choosing this flash card over feeling victimized—even if your partner forgot your shampoo and allergy medicine and seems totally unwilling to relate to you.

Your undefended candor will disarm your partner and be a responsible acknowledgment that you did something that might, in fact, upset someone. Probably he will say something like, "No, I don't hate you, I love you . . . that's why I feel so awful when I disappoint you." But even if he says, "Yes. Right now, I do hate you," *that, too, will be a relief.* Because once it's spoken, you will both instantly feel how human—and narrow-bandwidth—such "hatred" is. Innocently asked, *"Do you hate me?"* is a very friendly, and surprisingly bonding, question.

37·

I think I'm supposed to know how to do this, but honestly, I have no idea.

A number of years ago I had an emergency session with what I might have called an immature young couple from Argentina who were arguing with each other daily. I spent two hours with them going over the importance of *really* listening. I found out from the referral source that they deemed me "a true lifesaver."

Less than forty-eight hours later, I had one of the most primitive arguments ever with my own husband at the time—made worse by us screaming at each other between two floors—and was horrified to discover that the South American husband had dropped by to pick up eyeglasses he had left in my home office and heard every miserable word. I remember wanting to somehow blame my husband or explain, "I was only trying to manage an escapee from our in-patient psychiatric facility."

I bare my soul to you thusly in order to let you know that when we are triggered, we can all be immature. I'm sure the Universe orchestrated this humiliating situation to keep me humble. And while on a good day I can be quite in touch with myself and my present partner in sensitive, kind and skillful ways, there are certain interactions where I have said things with certainty and ten minutes later have totally lost my ground, where I have apologized for something I later saw was just making nice, where I was going on about something that I knew was self-indulgent and still couldn't stop, where I was trapped in grim gridlock feeling bored, boring and unable to connect.

Look at it this way: Do you think your parents, let alone grandparents, ever really gave much thought to whether they were having an "authentic" interaction with each other, whether they were "connected to their own insides" and "creating space for the Other"? We are all beginners in the intimacy department.

It will be a sign that you are in reality when you happily connect to this flash card.

38.

I feel like a total and complete idiot.

Let me just start by saying that unless your partner is from some yet undiscovered planet, this card is virtually foolproof if you want to melt their heart after you've said or done something insensitive, hapless, insane . . . or completely idiotic.

Once a mentor of mine did something incredibly generous, unasked for and unnecessary, along the lines of going to bat for me when I was in a tough situation and in need of a spokesperson. I was so deliriously happy about what he had done for me and the result that I e-mailed him, praising him to the heavens, and wrote: *"What can I ever do to repay you?"* And I was crushed when he took me literally and wrote back with three things I could do to repay him, one of which would have required literally hours of tedious work. After mulling over for days this somewhat embarrassing and icky predicament, I finally wrote him back that the gift he gave me was so precious and made me feel so taken care of that if I had to pay him back, I would need three months in rehab to work it all through . . . and was there some other way we could handle this?

Immediately upon realizing what he had done and the position he had put me in, the mentor—really a sensitive and sweet man—wrote back that his "narcissistic personality disorder subself" must have been the person who responded to my initial thank-you. And in 24-point type he wrote:

I feel like a total and complete idiot.

All gone. Like totally. As I said . . . foolproof.

PART IV

Taking
Responsibility

n order for two people to be in what I call "conscious relationship" with each other—particularly when there is conflict—each of them must have some awareness of the same four things: how I am feeling inside; how you are feeling inside; how you look to me on the outside and how I look to you on the outside. Most of us are excellent at the "how you look to me" module (e.g., critical, oblivious, smirking, disappointed in me, relentless) and not too bad at "how I am feeling" (diminished, pissed off, unfairly treated, fed up, walking on eggshells or some other form of nervous). What we usually aren't fabulous at is "how you are feeling." And we are often grossly out of touch with "how I look to you."

The flash cards in this section are designed to jog your awareness of these last two roads less traveled and to support you in appreciating more the impact your sub-wholesome behavior might be having on your partner. To take ownership of your overreacting or your relentlessness or your scariness—or even to take ownership of the possibility that you have a blind spot regarding your impact on your partner—is a beautiful and healing thing. This is what, at the end of the day, builds trust. And if trust isn't everything, it's almost everything.

A couples session stands out in my mind in which a young husband couldn't let go of the fact that when he stubbed his toe in the middle of the night going to the bathroom and cried out, his wife remained immobile and said nothing comforting. The wife insisted she must have been asleep—not the most bizarre alibi at three in the morning—but the husband could not let it go. He *knew* she had heard him. As I was about to offer him some therapeutic version of "enough already," the wife took a deep breath and confessed, "I wasn't asleep. I did hear you. I was drained from the day, worried because I had to get up early for work and wasn't feeling very nurturing. I am so sorry . . . and I can see how un-taken-care-of you must have felt."

To his credit, he simply smiled at her and said, "I love it when you just tell the truth."

And I suspect that the love and trust in the room at that moment was far beyond what it would have been if at three o'clock in the morning she had been Florence Nightingale.

39.

I can see that I've missed the point. Please give me another chance.

Dana was attempting to share with her husband her joy and amazement that a roadside worker had actually followed her six miles in heavy traffic to return her wallet, which he had found on the highway. She had absentmindedly left it on the roof of her car while opening the car door and then driven off. When she had finished telling her story, Mark immediately launched into a lecture on how careless she'd been to leave the wallet on her roof and reminding her of several other screwups in their life together that he was now more convinced than ever were signs of his wife having a serious "spacing out" problem.

NOT GOOD! This kind of scenario creates more intractable friction between couples than just about anything else. Mark was focusing on the content of what had occurred, using it as an opportunity to put forth his own long-standing agenda regarding Dana's slipups. He likely did this because moments like these—when she has done something careless such as forgetting to pick up his shirts—trigger his own early wounding around being seen and cared for. But he has indeed missed the point, and it makes Dana murderous. Why murderous? Because Dana is sharing something truly beautiful about a random act of kindness . . . something that reflects her highest ideal of how life should be lived—and her husband's incongruent response brings up deep fears that no one can share her reality . . . that she will never truly be met where she longs to be met.

When Mark held up this message acknowledging that he had missed the point, Dana's happy heart skipped a beat as she suddenly was able to appreciate her husband as much as, if not more than, she appreciated the good citizen who returned her wallet (which is how we usually feel when we see someone going the extra mile on our behalf).

Though it felt like a tricky message to put in this book, Dana could have made up her own message to flash to Mark: *"I hate you right now. Can you figure out why?"* You'd be amazed how the seemingly clueless then get it.

40.

I can see that my anger has been destructive and that I've really hurt you.

This flash card is a clear, straightforward example of taking responsibility for one's own negative impact on another. On the face of it, there's nothing very fancy here. Only we are so used to people either denying their anger or justifying it that the experience of an actual human being neither denying nor justifying but instead focusing on the harmful ramifications of their anger—*and on Thou, no less*—can border on the holy.

Clients say to me all the time, "Wouldn't you say I have *the right* to be angry?" "Wouldn't you be angry if your wife lent a friend twenty-five hundred dollars out of a joint savings account without telling you?" "Wouldn't you be angry if your husband promised to keep your four-year-old on the sleep schedule you valiantly hammered out, and then did what he damn well pleased when you were away on a business trip?"

Yes, I likely would be disappointed and quite possibly angry. But I have learned through seeing how my anger has hurt people I care about and by breaking through the seductive illusion that my anger is just good ol' me telling the truth, that anger is not something I should want "the right" to.

You might worry that in taking ownership of the harmful piece, your partner won't see what you are legitimately protesting or lobbying for (after all, lending someone $2,500 without discussing it with your partner is not great and messing up a four-year-old's hard-won sleeping schedule *is* looking for trouble) but that's not what this card is about. This card is about taking responsibility for your violent reaction and acknowledging that it was dealt not in the spirit of fostering understanding but from harmful entitlement. All I can say is that the more *you* trust you deserve to be seen, to be taken seriously and to be loved, say, while setting a boundary with your beloved, the less you will have to clobber your partner with "what's legitimate."

41.

I realize I'm overreacting.
Can you give me
a minute to get
sane again?

Sometimes in a relationship one party does something that drives the other person crazy. That's just how it is. The question is how to survive these moments without doing irreparable harm to your relationship, and one of the best ways to do this is to PAUSE AND TAKE A MOMENT TO GET SANE. Take a look at the following two reactions Talia might have in response to some interesting news from her husband:

(A) Talia: "You are *what*? Getting your ear pierced at age fifty-one? Are you for real? I think you passed the hippie statute of limitations long ago, Lenny. You're also too old for a midlife crisis. Seriously . . . don't you think you are being a little pretentious?"

(B) Talia: "I admit it gave me a jolt to hear that you are thinking of getting your ear pierced. I am so sorry I shamed you. I immediately flashed on my older sister giving you the business, and I imagined how embarrassed I'd feel when we see them next month. I know it's my problem caring what Rebecca thinks. Tell me . . . I'm genuinely curious—what made you decide to do this now?"

So how can you nip A in the bud before it tears everything you have with your beloved apart and get quickly to B? The answer is time, and that is where this flash card can be very useful. By acknowledging that you responded in an insane way and asking for a moment to get sane, you are signaling to your partner that—despite your horror at what they've done or propose to do—the last thing you want to do is hurt them or your relationship.

Let this flash card hold your place for as long as it takes for you to get in touch with your underlying sanity.

42.

I know I've been relentless. I can understand why you'd want to get away from me.

Simply put, this flash card allows you to get out of your own way and enter someone else's frame of reference. What does that really mean, though—*getting yourself out of the way*?

To me, it means letting go of any investment in your self-image and becoming *very* interested in little else but What's True. This is the magic formula underlying most of the flash cards in this book, and relationship healing in general—and this flash card, in particular, hits you over the head with the sheer beauty of it. The Sender is more or less saying, "I acknowledge I have been impossible and my energy has been aversive. It makes total sense that I have turned you off and that you wouldn't want to be near me."

The Sender has made herself totally ador-able because she has refused to do the obvious—make the Receiver feel small for fleeing. The Receiver will get this immediately and be most grateful, and there will follow a short period of disorientation—after all, the Sender has, unfathomably, transformed from an Invader into a Saint. The Receiver will now find himself in the slightly uncomfortable predicament of having no pre-existing response for such unabashed non-defensiveness. The couple's shopworn torture dance has come to a sudden halt, and neither of them knows quite what to do next.

Somewhere between awkwardness and gratitude, you will find your way. And I can promise you—at moments like this, you could do worse than to savor the awkwardness.

43.

I know I haven't made it very safe for you. Please don't give up on me.

While this flash card could likely find its legitimate place in any number of interactions, there is a specific circumstance where it is most recommended. This is when you have earnestly assured your beloved that you are truly interested in their perspective and promise to be a superb listener. You said things like: "Really, sweetie—tell me how it is for you," or "*Please*, I want to know," or, heaven forbid, "I know this is hard for you, but I want to make it safe for you." And then after two minutes of hearing something that annoyed you, sounded "unfair" or simply didn't seem to be getting to the point quickly enough, you got exasperated and let them know—in fact, let them know belligerently—that regardless of what they're feeling, they're out of their minds.

It happens all the time. Marv sincerely wants to hear how Beverly managed to total the car. Tearfully, she starts to tell the story, and thirty-five seconds into it, he sternly interrupts with, "*Well, were you or were you not* in the turn lane?" Janice can no longer ignore the fact that Gretchen has withdrawn from her for several days. She pleads with Gretchen: "Just tell me the truth—and I want to make it safe for you." But as soon as Gretchen tells her how left out and jealous she felt watching Janice so carefree with a new woman they recently met, Janice reacts as if she was being accused of disloyal behavior, and begins shaming Gretchen: "You give me no breathing space . . . I *knew* I shouldn't have talked to her in front of you!"

Writing this, I realize why I included "Please don't give up on me" on this flash card—it certainly is a sentence that could have enhanced a number of the messages in this book. When safety is hard to come by in a relationship—let alone when a promise of safety has been totally mangled—it would be natural to start giving up on one's partner. When the person who compromised the safety grasps the damage they have done, though, they will understand why someone might want to give up on them. And act accordingly.

44.

You are not being crazy.
I can see why you'd be
upset with me.

When we are feeling defensive, it's not exactly our conscious intention, but we tend to give our partners the message that they are, indeed, crazy for feeling as they do.

Victor asked Deirdre whether she knew the date and place of her niece's wedding. Deirdre replied, "I'll check for you later." Victor, agitated, yelled, "You didn't answer me!" Deirdre yelled back, "I said I'll check later." Victor, even more exasperated, said, "Can't you see . . . my question only required a yes or a no." Deirdre, feeling both strangely cornered and annoyed, asked, "What the hell is the difference?" And then added, "You are being crazy." The couple battled violently over this with Deirdre feeling bizarrely picked on and Victor beyond exasperated that Deirdre couldn't see the distinction he was making.

Okay, okay . . . Victor *is* sounding a teeny bit crazy putting so much energy into what is seemingly a minor semantic nuance. But not if you understand "we are never upset for the reason we think." As far as Victor is concerned, he grew up in a household where there was no such thing as a congruent response—people just free-associated or blew up. In this moment he wanted Deirdre to prove that he was no longer living in a terrifyingly chaotic universe.

Here's the truth: often when your partner is upset with you, a little part of them *is* crazy, if you consider the degree to which they are not aware of what ancient trauma is fueling their current one, they are not 100 percent "in reality." However, *your own need to see them as out of touch* may also come from a wound-based and, therefore, not-completely-in-reality place in itself.

In a perfect world, this is a card the Receiver might want to savor—and then flash back to the Sender. For Victor to have understood why he *was* sounding crazy to Deirdre would have made Deirdre feel very un-crazy.

45.

You are so upset, I probably don't fully understand my impact on you. Please tell me—I want to understand.

I sit here thinking of so many examples from my therapy practice and so many from my own life where this flash card would have felt like a breath of fresh nectar (a weird mixed metaphor, I know, but neither fresh air nor nectar by itself quite captures the thrill of it).

And I notice my reluctance to give you, the reader, my usual case material. Why? Because the humility and profound care this message implies shouldn't be wasted on anyone but yourself.

For most of you, you don't have to go back further than a week—surely no more than a month—to access a time when you were extremely frustrated by your partner's obtuseness . . . when you were deeply upset about something and just kept experiencing that, despite your best attempts, your partner didn't or wouldn't or just couldn't get it.

Now imagine how you would have felt if in the midst of this they had offered you the acknowledgment, "You are so upset, I probably *don't* fully understand my impact on you."

And continued with, "Please tell me—I want to understand." How dear is that!

Actually, this is the flash card that Deirdre, from the flash card before this, could have used to excellent effect when Victor was finding her helpfulness ("I'll check for you later") off-putting and her defensiveness anguish-producing. And she had no idea why he was making such a fuss, and it was sort of driving her crazy.

Humility, self-responsibility and love—all in one package. A breath of fresh air, nectar, an obtuseness solvent.

46.

I'm probably sounding like a parent right now, and I can appreciate that it's a turnoff.

f you've been paying any attention at all to life on planet Earth, not to mention your own relationship, it is pretty obvious that many things that are upsetting to you right in this moment are repeats of a childhood predicament.

The general patterns are familiar: parents who were controlling, belittling, distant, demanding, invasive, emotionally repressed, perfectionistic, forever worrying, overly security-conscious or occasionally overly disaster-conscious. There are thousands more specific themes like the mother who worried you were too bookish and not social enough . . . the father who conveyed you weren't smart or manly enough and would never amount to anything.

One of Freud's most far-reaching contributions was the discovery of an "unconscious," which determines much of our behavior, and the observation of "transference"—unfinished business from childhood authority figures that inevitably gets projected onto the psychoanalyst. Harville Hendrix, Ph.D., creator of Imago Theory, makes a convincing case that we will *always* unconsciously choose partners who have many of the negative qualities of our parents, with the higher purpose of this potentially horrifying fact being the precise need to kick up unfinished business so that unmet needs can finally be handled appropriately.

Well, the divorce rate tells you that this noble, if not God-given, mission is no walk in the park. And I'm making a point of it so you can have some compassion around the fact that the deck is already stacked against you: your partner is going to sound parent-like.

This is what makes this flash card so . . . well, respectful. It gets to the real root of not feeling related to as an equal, piercing the all-but-universal trance we get stuck in—that someone knows us or knows what's better for us than we do ourselves. The mature Sender can get their turned-off partner turned on quite rapidly with this flash card. Equality is where it's at.

47.

I was just reacting to you as if you were my mother, and I know that you're not.

nteresting, with all the controlling fathers in the world, that the phrase used more commonly when we're annoyed that someone seems to be telling us what to do is, "You're not my mother!" This also resonates with the popular assertion, "You're not the boss of me!" where there's an embedded suggestion that A Mother might even be entitled to be the boss of you. Let's face it—your first boss *was* your mother, and no matter how benevolent she was and even if you had a control freak of a father, it was usually your mother who told you: what to eat and when . . . which shirt is really "you" . . . why you should absolutely pee now, *before* getting in the car . . . who you should and shouldn't invite to your Bar Mitzvah . . . and what you must do before you can even think of leaving the house.

So it's no surprise that a part of us can feel quite bossed when our partners make even simple, reasonable requests: Will you call if you are going to be more than twenty minutes late? When you finish a roll of paper towels, would you remember to replace it with a new roll? The gas gauge is moving to a quarter of a tank—could you refill it now? Will you touch me there a little longer?

People of all sexes and sexual orientations can react to their partners as mother figures—and, believe me, further confounding reality, people of all sexes and sexual orientations can truly *act* like mothers, often impossible ones. Yet many of us entered our current relationship *already* a disempowered, if not disgruntled, employee of our first boss.

By offering this flash card, you are making the not insignificant distinction between being a tad bossy and "trying to be the boss of me." Making this distinction gives the Sender, though, the greater gift—getting a partner who is more of a friend than a drill sergeant.

48.

I was just reacting to you as if you were my father, and I know that you're not.

In my psychotherapy training there was a kind of wry, jokey question asked from time to time: What, really, was the point of the father? After all, it was always "the mother this, and the mother that . . . the overbearing mother, the cold, passive or seductive mother . . . Really . . . what *was* the point of the father?"

I remember one teacher of mine who had a very good answer: He said, "The purpose of the father is simply to help the child separate from the mother. And to this end, he must be neither too scary nor too unavailable."

While this is a gross simplification, and fathers in recent years have become far more nurturing, involved and "relevant," the teacher was saying something significant. We all start out in healthy symbiosis with our mothers and must hopefully move from being "Mommy-and-me" to thinking of ourselves as an individual Alice or Jerry or Madonna or Sting. While it's easy to blame our individuation failures on "the possessive mother," many of us sadly experienced our fathers growing up as scary or unavailable or both.

Shari freaked out because Bill totally forgot to pick up their sixth-grade daughter at school one day. Shari's upset was understandable ("What—do you think parenting genes come hidden in fallopian tubes?" she excoriated Bill). But the couple is never going to get through this moment unless Shari takes into account the impact of her own spacey father—legendary for the time her mother was making a Jell-O mold and needed an emergency can of crushed pineapple, and he returned from the supermarket with nine items, not one of them crushed pineapple. Here's the thing: Shari's intensity still has at least as much to do with her own father's lapses as with Bill's possibly troubling screwup. Really and truly.

49.

I'm probably
[sounding . . . looking . . .
carrying on] like your
mother right now, and
I can appreciate
how [frightening . . .
disturbing . . . annoying]
that must be for you.

While most of the messages in this book could have been worded in a hundred different ways (i.e., This feels awful . . . this feels terrible . . . this feels unproductive . . . , etc.), requiring me to make some highly subjective word choices, I feel called with this mother card and the following father card to give the reader a little multiple choice. Given the ease with which our partners can experience us as they experienced their parents, it is an act of intelligence and kindness to take the time to circle the most accurate words as a demonstration that you are really entering their world in a personal and aware way.

A little discernment here could go a long way toward helping your partner see that even though you can see that you do, indeed, "look" like his mother when talking about dieting while taking a second helping of mashed potatoes, the fact that you can understand how "disturbing" this is to him clearly distinguishes you from that diet-obsessed mother of his. When you realize that you've reminded her three times in the last twenty-eight minutes to pick up a pack of AA batteries when she is at Wal-Mart, it wouldn't hurt to acknowledge that how you are "sounding" could well be an "annoying" reminder of a certain female someone she grew up with. And, if her mother was an exacting schoolmarm and you blew up like a madman when she returned with the AAA double-pack, it might serve you to own the "frightening" and "disturbing" quality of your "carrying-on."

To offer this card is almost tantamount to one's mother coming to our twelve-year-old self and saying, simply and elegantly, "It wasn't you . . . it was me."

50.

I'm probably
[sounding . . . looking . . .
carrying on] like your
father right now, and
I can appreciate
how [frightening . . .
disturbing . . . annoying]
that must be for you.

Jen's father was an unruly alcoholic, and it was a constant source of pain for her that in her eyes, at least, her husband, Alan, occasionally drank too much. Unlike her father, Alan often went weeks, even months, without drinking. But a few times a year, almost always at social gatherings, he might have two or three drinks max, get a bit giddy, and Jen would threaten to leave him unless he promised to never have another drink. There were horrible battles over this, with Alan feeling grossly misperceived and Jen feeling that Alan had no idea what he was putting her through. For the record, this therapist, who can be a hard-liner on such matters, did not consider Alan a problem drinker.

For years, Alan pleaded, "I am not your father. I don't get drunk. Please get over this."

Several months ago, they replayed the same scenario at Jen's cousin's wedding. Only this time, Alan, now an owner of a set of flash cards, stopped defending his behavior and flashed to his wife upon arriving home: "*I'm probably looking like your father right now, and I can* [with the word *finally* added by hand] *appreciate how disturbing that must be for you.*"

I wish I could report that every flash card intervention had such a powerful and permanent result, but as of this writing Jen tells me that she is no longer threatened by Alan's occasional third glass of wine. This flash card was a hit with other couples in my practice. One husband's father was a compulsive gambler, and he would get triggered, not by a gambling wife but a bargain-hunting one. Something in her fervor to track down the cheapest airfare or the least expensive raisin bran felt like his dad's addiction (and probably was, to some extent). But the wife's owning how her behavior affected her husband allowed him to distinguish between a dangerous addiction and a quasi-compulsive sport.

51.

I'm probably acting like _____ right now, and I can appreciate how disturbing that might be for you.

Take your pick: the sadistic older brother . . . the cute attention-seeking younger sister . . . that lecherous uncle who wore a toupee . . . the ex who embarrassed you publicly . . . the ex who whined when you wouldn't have sex with them . . . the ex who spent evenings communing with their Black-Berry . . . the stepmother who treated you like a second-class citizen . . . the stepfather who was always so needy . . . the arrogant sibling or the condescending boss . . . the grandparent who preferred the brother who played the violin . . . The list is endless.

This card was originally designed for all the secondary characters, after parents, around whom you or your partner could have "transference" reactions. However, left to their own devices, users of these Flash Cards for Real Life have gotten rather creative: *"I'm probably acting like [a horse's ass . . . the Wicked Witch . . . Simon Cowell . . . Mother Superior] right now, and I can appreciate how disturbing that might be for you."*

However you fill in this flash card—and with flash card #52 following this, we have provided a second opportunity to fill in the blank—the beauty of this intervention is that you are taking it upon yourself to imagine how you might be seen by your partner. Even if he says, "Don't kid yourself, babe—not the Wicked Witch . . . we're talking more Saddam Hussein here . . ." something has been cracked and melted between you. There is definitely something to this taking responsibility stuff. To self-observe and show your partner you are genuinely *interested in* how they might be experiencing you . . . well, it might be worth it to acknowledge that you are starting to see the dictator or the martyr or the drama queen that lives in you.

52.

I'm probably acting like _____ right now, and I can appreciate how disturbing that might be for you.

See previous field note
(for flash card #51).

PART V

Giving Information

Whereas the flash cards in the "Taking Responsibility" section provide avenues for the Sender to maturely acknowledge their impact on their partner, the flash cards in this section are, for the most part, avenues for the Sender to candidly but nonabrasively let their partner know how their partner's stance is affecting them. They demonstrate the power of a good "I statement," a communication in which the speaker consciously takes ownership of their experience—especially their experience of you. Such statements let your partner know how they are coming across without all the extra baggage of accusation and assignation of blame that tends to accompany "You statements" (i.e., "You're putting me down"). The written format increases the likelihood of your dream come true— that you will get your partner to look at themselves, see their impact on you and . . . actually respect you for how you are handling something that feels off to you.

Current thinking in developmental psychology holds that an important component in the development of the most severe mental illnesses is the predicament of the child in a family where he lives in a barrage of double binds: he is told, "I love you" by a parent who puts out a hostile or even murderous energy. He is shamed for being dependent and shamed for acting independently. But the problem, clinicians believe, isn't in the double bind per se . . . it's in the taboo the child feels *to ever call the caregiver on the double bind*. While the impact of your childhood in this respect may not have led to serious mental illness in your own life, most of us are still struggling with the fact that we were either not allowed or not *able* to communicate how our parents' behaviors made us feel. By using the flash cards in this set when you are feeling confused, angry or upset by your partner's behavior, something automatically feels less crazy-making, usually for both of you.

To express, for instance, flash card #53: *"I don't feel heard,"* is to leave the double bind of continuing to interact with someone who some part of you knows isn't really listening. Flash card #61: *"Your behavior embarrassed me. I'm trying to tell you, not to make you feel bad, but so I can feel close to you again,"* puts on the table your suspicion that your partner is unable to see your positive intent. If this isn't addressed directly, both of you will continue to be defensive.

Our unspoken senses of things aren't always perfectly accurate and sometimes not accurate at all. But unaddressed, they make real intimacy all but impossible.

53.

I don't feel heard.

How much that is spoken between you and your partner that is less than pleasant might possibly stem from either or both of you feeling that a prior remark just wasn't received by the other? Eighty percent? Ninety percent? All of it?

Would there be conflict at all if we felt truly heard?

Once, a rare and enlightened husband I know listened so well when his wife confided that she found herself highly sexually attracted to a male colleague of hers, and she felt so heard by her husband about her plight, that she lost interest in the new possibility by nightfall and fell in love all over again with her spouse. I was about to say, "This isn't magic"—but actually, it is . . . only it's magic that is doable. I was about to say, "This isn't rocket science"—and it isn't . . . but it *is* counterintuitive, if you believe you have to "like" everything you are hearing. You don't have to like what you are hearing one bit to be a good listener. But what gets you over the hump and is worth cultivating is liking that your partner *wants* you to hear them.

If you have been clamoring for years for your partner to hear you, amassing evidence of their chronic failure in this department and the hopelessness of ever getting through . . . I can virtually guarantee that you will be delighted with the efficacy of flashing this nifty four-syllable message.

This flash card amazingly allows the deaf not only to hear—but to see.

54.

I know I'm pretty shut down right now . . . but I promise I'll be back.

Let me start by acknowledging that what I am about to say might sound a little bit abstract, but stay with me here a moment and consider this: There is no such thing as "having" a relationship with another person. There's only having a relationship with your own insides in that other person's force field. Let's say that prior to offering this flash card, the Sender, just home from work, said in an exasperated manner to their partner: *"How about giving me a moment before hitting me with your 'to-do' list?"* While somewhat abrasive, this is what passes in most homes as "having a relationship" with another person.

Now imagine that our home-from-work partner flashes a message that says, "I'm looking forward to sitting down and talking with you in an hour." And they are sincere about it. While better than the spoken statement above, why would it still be less satisfying than hearing, "I know I'm pretty shut down right now"?

Because the closer we get to sharing a simple undefended piece of our inner experience with our partner, the closer they will feel to us. The pretend flash card promising connection in an hour is, therefore, a nice attempt—but it won't produce the depth of intimacy we all crave. With our actual card, on the other hand, by sharing their internal state—in this case, their "shut-down-ness"—the Sender is treating their relationship with the person across from them as much more real.

All of this analysis may feel like putting legs on a snake but it is just this going inside ourselves that is so hard to do when, to stick with the current example, our world is telling us that we should be "up and at 'em" and "ready to relate," when the truth is, we are feeling depleted, contracted and even embarrassed by our shut-down-ness.

In the spirit of what I am saying here, feel free to amend this flash card: ". . . I promise I'll be back . . . but I can't promise when."

55.

I'm in knots. I'm afraid to tell you my truth, and it's horrible feeling that I have to humor you.

I've been pretending I'm looking forward to going to your company picnic. The truth is I hate bugs and making small talk, I'm dying for a pedicure, and I'm afraid you'll think I'm not being a true-blue friend . . . I've been pretending I'm okay with sending Katie to private school. My truth is: it is very expensive, I think the public school is excellent and I don't think the fact that you adored Aston Academy as a kid should be the dominant factor here . . . I've been pretending to be unfazed by your not going back to work, like you said you would, when Dylan turned three . . . I've been pretending not to notice that you seem so not-there when we're making love . . . I've been pretending to be okay with the fact that you've stopped going to your AA meetings . . . I've been pretending that it was okay with me that you went to your AA meeting and missed your daughter's ballet recital . . . It has felt so non-negotiable, I've been terrified to tell you that I really feel unmotivated to have a second child.

I'm afraid you'll find me disloyal, unsupportive, insensitive or plain contrary . . . but humoring you is killing me.

This is the basic drama of human differentiation, and taking off from the field note before this one, this is the place we often have to get to in order to stop making some idea of loyalty to you more important than loyalty to my own insides. This, in fact, is the beginning of real relationship—staying connected to my own insides in your force field.

Once you make yourself sturdier by *consciously* bringing your dilemma to your partner—the point of this flash card—you may happily find out that being perceived as disloyal, unsupportive, insensitive or contrary is not nearly as scary as having worried about it.

56.

I beg you to hear this as me truly wanting you to register my feelings—*not* as an attack on you.

Beg? Am I really choosing to use such a word in a compendium of conscious communication? I mean . . . beg?

It is so painful and, sadly, so common that honest, well-intentioned sharings get derailed because the listener feels personally attacked that we could say this book might be entirely unnecessary if that weren't the case.

Lonnie told Sal she was disappointed that he had failed to ask his boss for a raise, and Sal felt attacked. Hal told his wife, Robin, that he was upset with his fourteen-year-old stepdaughter for not doing more chores around the house, and Robin felt he was attacking her parenting. Bryna woke up and wished aloud to Grant that they had cuddled the night before . . . even acknowledging her own part in this . . . and Grant still felt attacked. Sometimes our partners will say, "You're attacking me," and sometimes they won't. But if they are defending themselves, like Grant, who said, glaring at Bryna, "I *told* you last night I was exhausted," it's a good guess that they are feeling attacked.

Your partner feels attacked largely because you make them feel bad about *themselves* versus about something that they did or failed to do. These are different things and yet the tendency to receive any kind of perceived criticism in this way is enormous. So what you are begging for is wanting them to trust that if they feel bad hearing you, that is *not* your intention. But make good on your promise and remember that you are asking them to hear your experience so you can feel known by them—not taking a shot at their dark side.

57.

You don't have to agree with me, but it hurts when you don't take me seriously.

If the issue is asking your partner to seriously hold space for a perspective different from their own, we recommend flash card #9: *"I don't need you to see this exactly as I do. But I do need you to hear where I am coming from."* This might be for when you want to argue the case for cutting your vacation short to make it to your niece's bridal shower. Flash card #55, however, has a different tone. It is for when you feel your partner is being superior, minimizing, humoring you, being cutesy or otherwise avoiding dealing. Like doing a shtick parodying the bride's gushing as she opens her shower gifts—trivializing bridal showers rather than dealing maturely with an understandable conflict.

To me, one of the most reliable principles in the inexact science of human relations is that people do not treat you the way you treat them—they treat you the way you treat yourself. So one of the reasons that any of these flash cards works so well is that the mere act of choosing to redirect a crummy interaction—key word here: *choosing*—elevates the relational vibe. The Sender is acting with self-respect by energetically declaring, "Enough with this crummy interaction!" And he or she usually is met with renewed respect.

This goes double for this flash card. Sticking with the bridal shower vs. vacation example, no one would blame you for getting exasperated at your partner's glibness. "Lee, just cut it out. If we are coming home for Jennifer's shower, we have to let the lodge know by tonight or we won't get a refund. Will you *please* get serious!" But imagine what it would mean if, instead, you flashed this message at Lee.

You'd be doing something novel. You'd be taking control. You wouldn't be seduced by Lee's humor, nor would you have to put energy into resisting him. You'd stop working to get his attention, and you'd be taking *yourself* seriously. And when Lee follows suit and drops his glibness, keep yourself a serious class act. Just say thank you.

58.

You didn't do anything wrong. I know it's my own craziness—trust me to get through it.

This we might call a companion card to flash card #44: *"You are not being crazy. I can see why you'd be upset with me."* The earlier message tells your partner that it is reasonable for them to be upset with you. It is truly entering their frame of reference and it is lovely validation.

But trust me—assuring your partner they aren't crazy won't be nearly as thrilling to them as assuring them that you actually know when you *are*. To have implied that your partner was insensitive, disappointing, misguided or generally bad and then withdraw your projection so cleanly will, at least in the moment, free your partner from any need *to keep proving that you are crazy.* In fact, they can take all the energy they were using to get you to see yourself and throw it into really liking you. It might make you nervous.

While this book was conceptualized largely for adult intimate relationships, this message is so on-point, wholesome and reparative, I strongly recommend flashing it to just about any child of yours who is old enough to read it. In fact, don't wait until your next bout of overkill. Just cheerfully reference your last one and flash accordingly. Your kid will get it instantly, be gratefully stunned and, as time goes by, be deeply appreciative of having been saved years of personal growth work to get validation for what they suspected to be true but couldn't fully trust.

My guess is that you could flash this card to a total stranger and they'd be somehow relieved.

59.

When you are so intense, it's hard to take in what might be valid about what you are saying.

Common wisdom exhorts us to "rather be happy than right"... but what if you really, really deep down really and truly *know* you are right? It's definitely a problem! The terror of not feeling heard when something really matters to us often causes us to call upon unnecessary intensity that tends to create just what we're dreading—not being heard.

There's a reason this book is called *Talk to Me Like I'm Someone You Love.* As mentioned earlier, we tend to hear the most abstract messages first, so if someone yells at us, "It feels *totally humiliating* having to call the contractor and tell him that we are changing the kitchen cabinets for the third time!" we are not going to be exquisitely attuned to or particularly care about our partner's legitimate vulnerability. It's more likely we are going to feel blamed for torturing someone, and respond self-protectively: "Well, *you* were the one who seemed so enthralled with the blonder wood when we visited the Milners!"

Intensity, by the way, comes in many forms, not all of them obviously combative.

Paula walked into a couples session with her husband, Don, and declared, "I say, 'I'm so excited!' and he automatically says, 'Oh, shit.' I tell him there's a fabulous movie I'd like to see, and he says it's the last movie he'd want to see. I bring home gorgeous carpet samples, and he says they're all ugly. If I'm enthusiastic, he resists me. I am not making this up."

Paula wasn't making it up, but she was out of touch with a piece. She had grown up with an extremely passive and depressed father, around whom she could rarely evoke a "Hi," let alone an "I'm so excited!" So when she would present her choices to Don, the desperate drumbeat was *"Do you like me? Can I make you happy? Excited? Please RESPOND!"*

I said to Paula, "Don isn't resisting you . . . he's resisting getting the enthusiasm test." This flash card is a nice way of letting someone know how aggressive they are being when they truly have no idea.

60.

You are taking up so
much space right now,
it feels like there is
no room for me.

can't tell you all the times I've worked with women in individual therapy who are bright, articulate, empathic, willing to look at themselves honestly and open to feedback, and somewhat miserable in their marriages with allegedly "sub-relational" husbands. They say things like, "I just can't get him to open up" and "He talks to no one . . . he has no friends . . . he barely makes small talk with his brother . . ." and "He's a decent guy, but his mother sucked the life force out of him . . ." and "He's terrified of feelings."

Often enough these reluctant husbands do make an appearance in therapy, and more often than not, this is what happens after I ask the husband how things are from his end:

Husband: It's been tough. I know Sharon is disappointed that we're not closer—but she's not the only one. We haven't made love in six months and I miss her. As a matter of fact—

Wife (*interrupting*): Haven't made love? And with whom would I do that? The man who missed his son's soccer game on Saturday?

And then I interrupt the wife and say something like, "I know you want your husband to engage more, and you deserve it. But for that to happen, he needs to feel safe opening up. And that means letting him know you are really interested in hearing his experience, even if it makes you uncomfortable, *even if it isn't the whole story."*

For those of you with a seemingly sub-engaged partner—and I'm certainly also addressing men here who wish their women would open up more—really take yourself on and ask, Do I do my part to open up the space for my partner or do I unwittingly close it up? For those of you who find yourselves in the position of the husband in my consulting room, give this flash card a try. It's a beautiful way to start reconstructing your rightful place in your relationship.

61.

Your behavior
embarrassed me.
I'm trying to tell you,
not to make you feel
bad, but so I can feel
close to you again.

It's hard telling your partner that their behavior embarrassed you. Usually you will choose to give them corrective feedback instead: "You did it again. You told them that whole golf-week-in-Scotland story, but you began throwing names around as if Gina and Matthew had a clue about who Miles Slater or Jay-Jay Crowe were. I saw them glaze over, trying to be polite. Your story was all over the place . . . even I couldn't follow you, and I've heard it fourteen times."

But usually such corrective feedback isn't helpful or well-meaning, and not surprisingly, it is poorly received. You're too angry at your partner for embarrassing you.

This flash card is for when you end up, say, haranguing your partner on the car ride home from the scene of your embarrassment. Long before you get home, you will know you did not behave well. You will try apologizing and actually owning up to your embarrassment, but by now, your intimate companion will be feeling too criticized and closed off to take you in. Go track down this flash card at once. This is when you can see how a written message can get through when words have already screwed you up.

62.

Your behavior was threatening to me. I'm trying to tell you about it, not to make you feel bad, but so I can feel safe with you again.

Let's look at what might be "threatening" to begin with. It might be threatening to walk in on your partner as they were addressing their unknown online bridge partner as "dear." It might be threatening to glance at the Visa bill and notice $1,800 in charges for guitar accoutrements after a serious "watching our spending" conversation. It might be threatening to see your partner sleep in when you thought they'd be at Home Depot by 8 A.M. getting supplies for an agreed-upon repair project. It might be threatening to watch your partner act like an FBI agent when your teenager comes home twelve minutes past curfew.

So let's be honest. Let's look at the part of you that wants to let your partner know how upset you are precisely because *you want them to feel bad*. Isn't it true? Because your whole life, people tried to get you to change by making you feel bad when your way of being threatened their security . . . It's the way of the world.

So I'll give you this—the examples above might be "good reasons" to feel threatened. Just notice, though, that you may also feel no different when your partner wants their car (theirs—not yours) to be desert beige instead of the usual white . . . when they tip the waitress a dollar more or less than you would have . . . when they sounded enthusiastic—but not enthusiastic enough—when your son hit a triple . . . when they wore a shirt to work that had a tiny stain on it. Notice how little it takes to feel your world is askew and how a part of you wants them to feel bad so they will stop doing something that makes you uncomfortable.

See if you can do this extraordinary thing: stay on your side of the net and tell your partner what is threatening to you, *from the perspective of just sharing something about your own reactivity.* Then they can enter your world and rather than defend themselves or modify their behavior at gunpoint, they can genuinely care that they rattled you.

63.

It feels like I can do
no right by you.

While relating can sometimes feel so complex that you need to be a combination of Jesus, Buddha, secretary-general of the UN and a communication expert to get it right, there really is an axiom that cuts through a lot. It is this: when someone really isn't liking you, you can do no right by them . . . and when someone is really liking you, you can virtually do no wrong.

This is the flash card to use when you sense your partner just isn't liking you, and this can range anywhere from not actively gunning for you to being absolutely unwilling to give you an inch.

Ralph and Terry weren't in a terrible space, but also not in a very good space before, during and after an informal dinner party they had at their house. They had bickered over whom to invite, whether to eat indoors or out, whether the background music should be Ella Fitzgerald or George Winston, and whether fruit salad was necessary with strawberry shortcake. After the party Terry

criticized Ralph for being too charming with the new neighbors they had invited.

"You were just too amusing and too attentive," said Terry. "You didn't pay enough attention to Roz, who could have used some attention since her husband left her. It's hard watching you when you're working to win over a crowd."

Ralph initially balked at his wife's indictment, and then stopped himself and replied thoughtfully: "You know, it's hard to hear, but I see some truth to what you're saying. To be honest, I think I spent so much time with them because they're looking for a new accountant, and I want the business. I probably was a bit too charming."

Terry replied, "You're just saying that because you think you'll win points with me for being non-defensive. I don't think you really see how you get."

Ralph has been a client of mine, and this is a true story. First of all, the Ralph of three years ago would never have acknowledged what was true in his wife's observation. The Ralph of a year ago would have been deeply offended by her invalidation and gotten hostile. The Ralph of two months ago walked out of the room, and came back holding up this flash card, *"It feels like I can do no right by you."* He did right by himself by refusing to continue to engage with someone who wasn't looking to see the good in him. And not surprisingly, his wife saw how *she* "gets," and began treating him with more heart.

PART VI

Getting
Clarification

These flash cards are designed to give you a much-needed boost when something really feels unfriendly or otherwise disconnected between you and your partner, and your tendency would be to have more of a relationship with the angst in your head than with your beloved. As uncomfortable as these times can be, they are opportunities to check out your worst fears, and your almost worst fears, with your partner in real time.

That being said, this is probably a good time to point out that there are almost always two versions of your partner available to you—the real one and the one in your head. Which one shall you choose? (Sobering to consider that these same options are open to your partner!)

Why make yourself sick worrying whether your partner is thinking of leaving you, doesn't really respect you, is annoyed beyond repair, hasn't the foggiest notion of what you have been imploring them about or, perhaps worse, is holding on to a truly foggy notion of what's been going on between you.

There is no relationship that couldn't benefit from about 250 hours of serious reality-testing. And one of the benefits of asking pointed questions is that your partner will be put in the position of having to take some real responsibility for the vibes they are putting out. Sometimes it's a question of calling them on their bluff.

There are many reasons why this book was created—and some might scoff at the idea of written flash cards deepening a relationship—but an enormous amount of "relating" is actually done with the characters in your life, not the least of whom is your partner . . . in your head. I hope the flash cards in this book, and the ones in this section in particular, will get you less interested in the beloved-who-frustrates-you living in your head, and more interested in the human being in front of you.

64.

When you treat me this way, it feels like you don't respect me. Is that true?

It can feel demeaning, if not humiliating, when someone who matters to us speaks to us as if we're stupid or inadequate, as if we're inferior or insufferable. Or snaps at us with minimal provocation, rolls their eyes at something we said or walks out of the room disdainfully when we are trying to initiate a conversation. Or lies there in bed, refusing to engage, because of a misinterpreted or mishandled sexual directive. (It can feel disrespectful when they seem to prefer to wallow in their "feeling offended" rather than do what they can to reinstate their connection with us.) But it can only really, really gnaw at you if you feel so ashamed of yourself that you are unwilling to look your partner in the eye and deliver the message above. If your partner is behaving disrespectfully, reclaim your dignity by looking them in the eye and *requiring them to take full responsibility* for their lack of respect in a direct and honest way. "Tell me straight, buster . . . if you really don't respect me, tell me straight, rather than let it leak out through your contemptuous behavior and superior tone."

Aligning yourself with this flash card helps you reclaim your dignity, because you are transmitting the self-respect of one who is not too timid to put the respect issue on the table. On top of that, the *"Is that true?"* has the energy of an innocent questioner.

How can you not respect, if not love, someone who only wants the Truth?

65.

When you say things like that, it sounds like you are thinking of ending our relationship. Is that what you really mean?

It's one thing to put on the table the question of whether, as in the previous flash card, your partner really respects you—a more "diffuse" concept to begin with—let alone whether your partner could respect you deeply and still feel you were a ninny when it came to how you handled the landscaper this morning. But whether or not they are thinking of ending the relationship is another whole order of things. Particularly if the context is adversarial, and your partner says something like, "I don't know how much longer I can put up with this," or states sadly, "I thought the differences between us wouldn't matter, but I was wrong . . ." I don't know whether you are hearing the most abstract message first or the most concrete, but it would be natural to hear these utterances as an implied threat of loss and for a part of you to feel panicked.

With all due respect to this book, I can appreciate that when the *Titanic* is sinking, your first thought might not be to grab this book—but make a mental note right now of the subtitle, *Relationship Repair in a Flash*, and the fact that it is designed for emergencies. What will come out of your mouth when you fear that your partner is thinking of jumping ship will probably not be helpful (i.e., "For chrissake—do you think it's been a picnic for me?"). And since there is a 97 percent chance that your partner is not really thinking of ending the relationship, why not let them know you will not interact with them with such insecurity and possible emotional manipulation in the space. So if they are really thinking of ending the relationship, let them stop torturing you and tell you their true agenda right this minute.

Like the child who cries, "I wish you were dead!," your partner is feeling overwhelmed.

If you are too unstrung to empathize with your partner's feeling of being overwhelmed when they implied they've had it with the relationship, go search the *Titanic* for this flash card.

66.

What can I say that would make you feel understood?

Pick an incident where you felt you just weren't getting through to your beloved, where it felt to you like you just wanted them to understand what from your end was one simple thing and they didn't seem to be registering it. Here's an example: "I'm trying to get you to see that when we're making love and something doesn't go smoothly, and you get frustrated and say something like, 'Well, it's obvious that you're just not that into it,' it feels like you are closing a door on us. I'd love it if at moments like that we could slow things down, reconnect, reboot and get in a new groove."

Maybe to you that sounds like one simple thing, but conceivably to your partner it sounds like a two-week-long relationship seminar. They respond with things like, "What's the point, if you're just not into sex with me?" or "I *asked* you what would feel good, and when I did what you asked, what happened—you seemed to fall asleep!" or "Does everything have to be processed to death? So we had a lousy sexual experience . . . Leave it alone." And so on.

It's tense between the two of you, and you've been trying to process this for a while, not particularly successfully, when your partner, to their credit, sighs and asks, "Okay, what *can* I say that would make you feel understood?" But . . . hear the muted exasperation in their voice, the unspoken "all right already" preceding the attempt to give you a better experience. As mentioned, when we are not relaxed, it is *very* hard to free our voice of contaminating unsavory tonals.

Now imagine your partner just proffers this flash card—hopefully with a kind expression on their face. No pesky tone of voice cluttering the works. No thinking on your part, "They're just trying to shut me up." No feeling weirdly pressured to come up with an answer that will make everything perfect.

Can I tell you what usually happens? The Receiver feels so loved that the Sender *cares* to get it right that he or she may not even need to clarify their original misunderstood communication. Feel into why this is so. It is profound.

67.

Tell me the truth—am I responding in the way you need me to right now?

Betsy was trying to tell her husband, Ned, that a few evenings ago when she was in a lousy mood, she just needed some space to complain about how miserable she was. Her colleague at work was in a serious car accident, adding to her workload, she was unsettled because her older sister wasn't returning her e-mails and she wished Ned would bring his snack dishes from the den into the kitchen.

The point Betsy was making about all this was that it annoyed her that Ned's way of responding to her distress was to become her "assertiveness coach." Ned made an effective case that Betsy's work problem was *exactly* the same problem she was having with her sister, not to mention her ex-husband—her chronic inability to set boundaries. And he wanted to role-play with her "standing up for herself."

Now, in this follow-up interaction, Ned was trying to be a better listener. "Hmmm, so let's go back to Thursday night. You didn't want any advice . . . or is it that you wanted less advice? And I did ignore the dishes issue. I promise you, honey, I am going to be a better cleaner-upper. And maybe I don't get what it means that Corrine has been out of the office." And so on.

Betsy, who, to be honest, does have "boundary issues," including with Ned, felt stymied. Her husband was trying, but something was still off. They both felt it. To his credit, Ned asked, *"Tell me the truth—am I responding in the way you need me to right now?"*

Betsy said, "No, you aren't." Ned said, "Tell me more." Betsy said, "I would have felt loved if you had just said, 'It makes sense to me that you felt unsupported by me Thursday night.'" And Ned hit a home run when he said, "It makes sense to me that you felt unsupported Thursday night, and it makes sense that you felt unmet by me a few minutes ago when you were trying to tell me about it." How a real vignette from my practice inspired a flash card.

68.

Are you in the
space to talk?

So simple, so respectful, so effective and so very underutilized.

If you, reading this, are the partner who tends to be the one more eager for contact when there is tension between the two of you, this flash card could change your life. I make such a dramatic claim because I am betting that *your* partner, the one who tends to distance, has little expectation of you being so respectful of their boundaries when you are wishing you could be closer. They are expecting you to talk *at* them, demand, cling, repeat yourself and act like their not relating to you is consigning you to an Alaskan ice floe.

Look at it this way: the mere fact of offering this flash card contains the meta-message: "I get that to get into this with you *without* asking first would be unwelcome, if not invasive." So the Receiver feels accurately perceived—finally—as *a Being needing boundaries, not as a Depriver of Connection*. For many of you reading this, such a turnaround could be a very welcome and wholesome way of looking at something.

I am making such a big deal out of this, not because I believe your ability to respect boundaries has been so terrible, but because I suspect most everybody is at least somewhat lacking in this area. Just about anyone who has ever been a child has experienced having their territory more or less invaded. Most of us were certainly not asked: "The laundry needs to be taken out of the dryer and folded. Is this a good time for you to do it?" or, "Your hair seems to be getting longer than usual. Do you want to cut it or just let it grow?" or, "There's something I've been wanting to talk with you about. Are you in the space to talk?"

69.

You seem so [prickly . . . defensive . . . enraged] that I feel pulled to do or say anything to calm you down. Is that what you really want?

A while back (flash card #54) I suggested, "There is no such thing as 'having' a relationship with another person. There's only having a relationship with your own insides in that other person's force field." This flash card enables you to make this principle explicit with your partner.

When we respond to our partner's anger, upset or defensiveness by walking on eggshells around them, we are, in effect, betraying our "insides" or, in other words, ourselves. And while walking on eggshells is the norm for many couples, having to do it at all is, if you think about it, very sad.

This flash card puts the issue most central to the maintenance of a conscious versus unconscious relationship on the table. You are asking your partner, *Do you really want me to be "loyal" to you at the expense of being disloyal to myself?*

It may feel counterintuitive to put your soul in the hands of someone who isn't doing a very good job right now in the self-soothing department, and wants you to help calm them down, not put them in a moral quandary. But consider this: asking your partner to consider whether they really want you to de-self on their behalf is inviting them into their aware and thoughtful Self and out of their self-protective one. What a beautiful way to wholesomely help them calm down.

70.

I can absolutely see why you'd be annoyed with me, but can you give me some sign that we're still friends?

Obviously, you would be inclined to flash this message when you know you have done something annoying . . . like doing something you explicitly agreed not to do (e.g., buying drop-dead-gorgeous but really overpriced carpet, taking an overweight child to lunch at McDonald's, divulging something embarrassing about your partner) or *not* doing something you promised to do (e.g., picking up supplies for a child's life-and-death school project, visiting your mother-in-law, calling back the financial planner regarding a time-sensitive matter). Maybe you annoyed them by flashing flash card #68: *"Are you in the space to talk?"* and they gave you an unequivocal "No," and you spoke your mind anyway.

I like this flash card because my whole adult life I have been exploring the question: How do you hold ruptures and upsets in a larger container of friendliness? Yet . . . the Sender of this message is also being called upon to balance three things: (1) the self-worth inherent in knowing that even Those Who Annoy deserve love, (2) the anxiety inherent in knowing one has, indeed, transgressed and, let's not forget (3) the Receiver's lawful right to be irritated—at least, for a bit. What I am saying is that this card shouldn't be flashed too quickly in the process just because the Receiver's annoyance is intolerable to you. This would require the Annoyed to leave their own feelings too quickly in order to reassure you. Give them a little time to be upset with you.

Flash this card when you really trust that your current annoyance is approaching what would be some universal statute of limitations. Don't flash it just because you fear you may have done something that could forfeit someone's goodwill toward you. Flash it when you genuinely believe you deserve to be considered a true friend despite a passing moment of insensitivity, passivity or flakiness.

71.

It would mean a lot to me if you could just repeat back to me what you think I'm trying to get across.

Given how fervently most of us want to be heard by our partners, it is interesting to me how infrequently we simply ask for evidence that our communication has "landed."

Sure, you *could* just verbally ask your partner to repeat back to you what they think you are trying to get them to understand. But, sadly, somehow the verbal request is often experienced as "an instruction" or a criticism or some interference in the flow of the ongoing interaction (even if everyone would agree that things thus far haven't been very flow-y!). There's something about being given the request via written message that demonstrates some seriousness of purpose. Users report that it feels respectful and that the Receiver feels called upon to meet a need, as opposed to having to do something to make up for previous substandard listening. Almost always, the Receiver rises to the occasion.

Jenna and Mason had been to a couples communication workshop where Mason balked at having to repeat back to his wife what he heard her say. "It feels so stilted," he complained—and he is not alone feeling this, though if questioned, most complainers will agree that "stilted" is usually an improvement over "defensive" or "all over the place."

The couple was having a very difficult conversation about a difficult topic—adopting a child who was not Caucasian, like they were. Jenna, desperate for a child, felt it was small and withholding on Mason's part to limit their options because of race. Given that they had been through years of unsuccessful infertility treatments, Jenna, at age forty-one, felt there really wasn't much need for discussion, and felt angry at Mason for putting "one more obstacle" in the way of her and motherhood.

Jenna was discombobulated further when it was Mason who reached for their book of flash cards and held up: *"It would mean a lot to me if you could just repeat back to me what you think*

I'm trying to get across." Mason noticed he didn't care that much that Jenna was all but parroting his considerations back to him. There was something about holding up the card that he felt required his wife to *see* that beyond the compassion he had for her, there were still two realities in the room.

PART VII

Apologizing

· · · · · · · · · · ·

· · · · · · · · · · ·

grew up in a generation in which the line from *Love Story* (the 1970 film with Ali McGraw as a dying Radcliff student married to a Harvard jock played by Ryan O'Neal) "Love means never having to say you're sorry" was a household phrase. As someone who has, over the years, quoted this line rather mindlessly many times, the writing of the introduction to this particular grouping of cards felt like a good occasion to explore whether I actually believe it. But first I polled a number of people, most of whom seem to agree with my beloved, who stated simply, "It's rubbish."

He is a man who walks his talk, and truth be known, I do like it *a lot* when he says he is sorry . . . and it does make me feel loved. But I don't think I like it as much as I do just because it is a wonderful gift (which it is) or even because it can feel like a deserved acknowledgment that he has caused me some measure of pain. I deeply appreciate a sincere apology because it is such a beautiful expression of both vulnerability and responsibility-taking—I feel loved because my guy is willing to own something less than honorable about himself with the intention of keeping *himself* clean. And in the end, I get something even better than being loved—I get to love a man I see as honorable. The flash cards in this section provide eleven opportunities to take something that transpired between you and your partner that was petty, mean-spirited, hurtful or just plain thoughtless, and turn the moment into something honorable.

Thinking more about the *Love Story* quote: it probably also alludes to the idea that real love means trusting that your beloved *already* feels so much sorrow for any pain caused that a verbal expression of their remorse—the apology—is redundant or irrelevant. But to me, it's not the requirement of an apology or lack thereof that says much about the love between two people. It's that real love flourishes best between couples who are committed to letting nothing come between them, and for this . . . sometimes words are what's called for.

72.

I'm sorry.

Unlike that other short and sweet statement, "I love you," I have found that a verbal "I'm sorry" has a much better chance of getting drowned out in a tough interaction. Perhaps this is because "I'm sorry" or plain "Sorry" is spoken so frequently and automatically—bumping into a stranger, accidentally getting ahead of someone in an ATM line, calling a wrong number, reaching for the same package of portobello mushrooms as a fellow shopper—it sometimes just doesn't carry the oomph one might like when expressed verbally.

I love you," on the other hand . . . Though my research hasn't been extensive, it's been conclusive: verbal "I love you's" are ever-popular and ever-heartwarming, while a written "I love you" in the midst of an argument tends to come across as merely a lame attempt to appease one's partner or stop the unpleasantness. The "I'm sorry" flash card, on the other hand, is an interpersonal show-stopper. I suspect this is because when you've hurt or offended your beloved, they want to know *that it bothers you*. In this moment, your partner probably doesn't need to know that you love them as much as they need to know that you care that what you did or failed to do had an impact on them. And this is one card where you don't have to worry if it takes you a moment of fumbling with this book to find it. By all means take your time. There seems to be something about the very act of hunting down this flash card and quietly flashing *"I'm sorry"* that carries an undertone of penance with it. Indeed, if you are like most people confronted with the truth that an apology is, in fact, called for, your first reaction is to point out to your partner that if they knew the larger context, your deeper motivation or that Mercury was retrograde at the time, they would see things differently. In which case this flash card will be experienced as both an apology for the original grievance *as well as* an acknowledgment that it took far too long for you to apologize.

73.

I know I've really hurt you. What can I do that would help you trust me again?

Notice that this flash card doesn't say, "What can I do to make up for it?" or "What can I do to help take the pain away?" This is because when your partner has really hurt you, the thing that most urgently needs repair is the rupture in trust that has occurred. We all possess a deep-seated wish that the people who love us will never hurt us. Period. The fact that the Sender is bringing trust into the equation at all will make the Receiver open to the possibility that the Sender is capable of appreciating the gravity of the situation. This flash card is generally contraindicated for devastating hurts where moral lines have been crossed—sexual, financial and other ethical indiscretions come to mind. In these moments in a relationship it is important to realize that trust needs to be rebuilt, and that it may take time. In asking the Receiver to help design a "trust plan," the sender of this card is acknowledging this fact. But extreme cases aside, most

couples can easily hurt each other several times a week. Frequently the hurt has to do with not feeling truly received by the person who matters most to you.

Carrie was in the bathroom brushing her teeth when Jonathan walked in. Carrie grinned at him lovingly in the mirror and for whatever reason, Jonathan missed her bid for connection and joked, "Looking at yourself again? How narcissistic!" Carrie shut down and Jonathan was mystified that his playfulness had such a negative effect. After twenty minutes of raised voices, Jonathan grabbed flash card #73. Carrie felt safer, and said, "It hurt that you didn't see I wanted to make eye contact with *you*. Can we go back to the mirror? I want to look at you again, and I want you to just smile back—and no smart-ass remarks."

The content in this incident might strike you as too minor to initiate a trust-building endeavor. But it's not the content that ruptured trust in the first place. In the incident above, Jonathan triggered an ancient button in Carrie around her desire for connection going unrecognized. And more often than you would expect, an effective way to rebuild trust is simply, Take 2.

74.

I know what I said was hurtful. I truly didn't mean it and would do anything to take it back.

We don't like to think of ourselves as being mean. It's much more satisfying to think we've said hurtful words because we were being "candid" or we were "telling it like it is." But all of us have the capacity to say mean things—things that serve only to hurt our partner and injure our relationship. Some things just shouldn't have been said. Period. For example:

"If your boss knew what you're like at home, he wouldn't have hired you." "How can I trust that you'll stay with this major home remodeling project? Look what you did with that gym membership." Or worse:

"If I'd known you'd be forty pounds heavier [or weren't more of a go-getter], I don't know whether I would have married you," or "It just doesn't feel like you are my equal," or "I never thought I'd be with someone so sexually unadventurous."

That there might be shards of truth and genuine disappointment behind these remarks doesn't keep them from being mean. If you care at all about your partner and the quality of your relationship, it would behoove you to acknowledge the mean piece, and that the only "thinking" going on when you said what you did was about yourself.

75.

I'm sorry that I've been acting as if everything's all your fault.

Anumber of years ago a woman drove more than a hundred miles each way, to be counseled by me because I came highly recommended and she wanted "the best." She said she needed crisis counseling, the crisis being her conviction that her husband was having "an emotional affair" with a woman, Toby, whom he e-mailed regularly through an online day-trading educational site.

Finally, after a few sessions, I said to her, "Look, the only one we really know is having a secret life is you—schlepping here undercover every week. Talk to your husband."

She called me a few days later. "I spoke to Jake and he was flabbergasted. He pointed out how I've moved into the guest room and have been sleeping with our cat. He said, 'It is you who has been having an emotional affair. I cannot compete with Buffy.'" It also came to light that this woman's need to have "the best" and be "the best" made it hard for her to believe that her husband could be coached by this advanced trader, and still

prefer her. It actually turned out that Toby was male—and the husband was not gay— meaning my client's fear that her husband had a romantic interest in Toby was pure projection.

I am not making this up. My client was a likable social worker who communicated well—only she never thought to mention "moving in" with Buffy. She only "knew" she was losing her husband. This is an extreme example—but notice that when something feels off in your relationship, one rarely asks, "How might I be *co-creating* this?"

This flash card is for when you notice that you've been blaming your partner for: the distance between you . . . your teenager's worst behavior . . . the fact that the vacation was awful . . . having either not enough sex or not enough alone time . . . or, whatever it is, *the other one* "started it."

Imagine how nice your life could be if you were both responsible and no one was to blame.

76.

I feel embarrassed about
how I spoke to you.

Under the right circumstances, a message like this one makes the otherwise powerful "I'm sorry" pale in comparison. In fact, it's a beautiful example of how an admission of vulnerability can become the ultimate love letter—how staying connected to your own vulnerability can deepen and authenticate your relationship with your partner. I toyed with adding a second sentence to this flash card: *"I feel embarrassed about how I spoke to you. You didn't deserve it."* But letting your partner in on your own embarrassment about how you treated them is unto itself a great, if not perfect, confirmation of what they deserve.

I like the idea of flashing this card as is and, following the energy of the moment, possibly adding a verbal "I'm sorry" or "You didn't deserve it" . . . or letting it stand alone.

Your partner doesn't "need" you to feel embarrassed for a rupture to be repaired. They just need to know how much you want them to know the real you.

77.

Please—can you forgive me?

Whole treatises have been written on forgiveness. It is one of the cornerstones of all religions and a big agenda item in the world of psychospiritual seeking. It is the cornerstone of what may arguably be the most respected and long-standing growth training on the planet, the Hoffman Quadrinity Process, in which thousands of participants come regularly to do everything possible to forgive their parents and get on with their lives. *A Course in Miracles*, which has sold close to two million copies and been translated globally, makes a compelling case that our sole function on earth is to forgive anyone who triggers us—and that this is the only way we will heal ourselves. Twelve-Step programs make a point of making amends to others and working on self-forgiveness. Most couples therapists would agree that for a couple to put an extramarital affair behind them, the betrayed partner needs to not only forgive their spouse, but often acknowledge the subtler ways he or she may have co-created the betrayal.

All this is to say that you don't have to worry about whether or not, in the ultimate scheme of things, you deserve forgiveness. You do. But in terms of this book and this flash card, the question is: When?

The giving of a written message like this is a potentially sacred act, and it would be sacrilegious, if not manipulative, to hold up this request in an effort to merely get your partner off your back. This is for when you have done something really lousy, have truly allowed your partner to have their feelings about it—even extended feelings about it—and now know in your heart of hearts that you truly feel remorse.

In other words, the key variable that might move you toward this flash card isn't that your partner won't let it go. It's that your partner won't let it go AND your remorse is so sincere that you truly believe you deserve their forgiveness. No cheating.

78.

Even though I've been arguing my position like a crazy person, I now see where your point of view makes sense.

Roberta, an interior decorator and friend of mine, shared the following story with me: "Twenty-five years ago when we were buying our first house, I was so excited that I had found 'The One' that I tracked down my husband at a restaurant and took him immediately to look at a property which had amazing moldings, a living room with a high ceiling, a kitchen with original bread warmers and a third-floor bedroom and bath—all for thirty thousand less than we were prepared to pay. He seemed to love the house as much as I did, but kept insisting we couldn't possibly buy it. He kept saying, 'Don't you know, you are *never* supposed to buy a house on a corner?' For three days this normally flexible man was unmovable, citing noise factors, water mains, resale concerns and traffic patterns that could have been the migration trajectory of Norwegian salmon, it all felt so irrelevant to me. I had more than one tantrum, and finally begged him, 'Where did you get this idea—never buy a house on a corner?'"

And Leo, her husband, answered, "My father. He used to say it all the time." Roberta told me, "My father-in-law was a builder, so he knew something about houses . . . but he also was a man who believed Sputnik was a hoax, refused lifesaving medicine and required eight-year-old Leo to document every last penny of his quarter allowance. This would not have been someone I'd have chosen as a consultant."

Often when we've been arguing our position like a crazy person, it's precisely because we aren't that grounded. This was a case where Leo—like all of us at times—was more fused with his parent's reality than his own. Having watched Roberta and Leo over the years, I can say there were many times both of them could have used this flash card with each other. And they are no different from you and your partner and me and mine.

79.

I'm sorry I made such a big deal out of something so unimportant.

The truth is, one can also make too big a deal over something important—Should we move to Seattle? Confront your brother about his pot addiction? Try in vitro fertilization?—if what we are talking about is hysteria, jumping to conclusions, turning everything into a catastrophe or your basic blowing things wildly out of proportion. For these, try flash card #41: *"I realize I'm overreacting. Can you give me a minute to get sane again?"*

When I created this flash card I admit I had forgotten that #13 is very similar: *"I was making a big deal out of something that just isn't that important. I want to let it go."* But after much soul-searching, I'm including both of them, and here's why: the former flash card is in the first section, "Shifting Gears," and the *"I want to let it go"* implies that the Sender is reporting they are in process with something—not quite there yet but en route. But notice, it really doesn't *feel* like this later one does. The Receiver hasn't been let off the hook yet.

Comparing the two flash cards, you can see that there's something to this apologizing. Probably, if you were moved to use this card, you were making your partner wrong for something that wasn't a character flaw: not sounding cheery enough when you asked them to run an errand for you . . . moving the car insurance bill from point A to point B on your desk . . . asking you, "Do you really need it?" when you were perusing the dessert menu. They made you feel bad . . . and now you have made them feel bad for making you feel bad. Most of this is done unconsciously. Not to wax macrocosmic or anything, but this is the process that causes wars.

This flash card puts the badness in its place. You are consciously owning a little piece of badness and freeing your partner from feeling they did such a horrible thing. This is what enlightened masters do. Putting things in perspective is the road to world peace.

80.

You have no idea how much I regret the direction I took this in. I'm really sorry.

Many years ago I was close to being engaged to a man who had an office in a building next to mine. One freezing January evening I had a client in acute suicidal distress, warranting an emergency session. I rushed to my office and, admittedly, parked in a nearby handicapped parking spot so as not to leave the client waiting too long. When I came outside at 9 P.M. in 11-degree weather, I had not one but *two* slashed tires and an obscene note from a handicapped person on my windshield. Now, almost as distressed as the client I had just finished with, I ran to the office of my boyfriend and burst into tears, simply feeling the violence of what had occurred.

"What's with you?" he began. "You *know* you're not supposed to park in handicapped spots." I got upset and replied, "I KNOW I'm not supposed to park in handicapped spots. But you're not allowed to tell me that until you first tell me, 'I'm going to prowl the streets right now, find the little tyrant and let him know you were saving a life in there, and then beat him up.'" I was joking, of course (at least partially), but I wanted him to see that he was heading in the wrong direction with me in that particular moment. We've all done it. Your partner tells you how impossible their boss is, and you reply flippantly, "This problem with your boss keeps showing up because of your male authority issues, and until you deal with them, it will keep showing up." Stop! Turn around! The point is that the wrong direction is often offering opinions, judgments or even the holy Truth—before offering empathy and support. For many moments like the one reported above, my almost fiancé remained an almost. This flash card and the awareness behind it might have made a very big difference.

81.

I'm so sorry I couldn't
hear you sooner.

This is a flash card that has the potential to make your partner feel deeply felt and cared for. It expresses so much more than just regret for putting them through hell before finally "getting" what they were saying. With very few words, this flash card tells your partner, "I'm sorry I forced you to live in this world one minute more than you had to feeling you weren't making sense to someone who matters so much to you." It acknowledges how painful it must have been for them all that time they were *trying to get through to you*, and how they must have begun to doubt it would ever happen.

If, horrifyingly, you were buried alive, and someone later looked at you with tears in their eyes and said, "I'm so sorry I couldn't hear you sooner," you'd know that they were saying far, far more than "I'm sorry it took so long to get you out." There'd be an implicit awareness of the unendurable horror you were forced to experience until being rescued. While that's a to-the-nth-degree example, I believe it's an illuminating one. When we are desperate to get through to a resistant or merely tone-deaf partner, it can feel like we are being, if not buried alive, close to it. It doesn't matter that we got our best friend or officemate or yoga teacher to perfectly understand why, say, wanting to be alone for a day says nothing about our love for our partner . . . We need *our partner* to trust that what we are trying to say is very real for us, and that their not entering our reality is like a knife to the heart.

I thought of including in this book a flash card that says, *"You make sense to me."* But it felt weak and off-point. This one feels better because I believe that what we are really yearning for isn't affirmation that we make sense—but for someone to grasp the anguish we feel when it feels impossible to make our experience make sense to someone we love.

82.

I'm sorry that I acted
as if there was only
my reality.

Sometimes I do a therapeutic enactment where I ask a client to imagine he is a three-year-old building a tower with imaginary blocks. I role-play "Mommy A," who rushes up to him, grabs his arm and says, "Hurry up . . . we have to get to Grandma's!" Then I do a rerun as "Mommy B," who approaches him more slowly and says something like, "You are really working on that tower! I feel awful having to interrupt you, but I can't leave you here alone. I am so sorry . . . and there's *absolutely no reason right now why you would want to go anywhere.*" If I do this sincerely enough, more than half of my "three-year-olds" start to tear up. Many sob. It is the first time some part of them got a message that it was not a deal-breaker or "a problem" to have an emotional reality different from a loved one's.

So while many people can now assert that they grew up in a dysfunctional family with the likes of Mommy and Daddy A, most of us are still not spectacular being in a "dual-reality relationship"—in other words, any relationship with someone who isn't you.

Vera, an outgoing dance teacher, and her lower-key partner, Marcus, a sociology professor, were living in a large suburban development. One Sunday before having brunch on their patio, Vera, who was out cutting chives from the garden, started chatting with the new neighbor next door and spontaneously invited him to join her and Marcus. The couple's post-brunch conversation went something like this:

Marcus: Lou is a lovely man, but I wish you would have asked me first before inviting him over. I was looking forward to it just being the two of us.

Vera: It really bothers me hearing you say that. It felt so good just being able to be friendly and not have to "get permission." I want you to let me be me.

Marcus: It has nothing to do with

letting you be you. I wouldn't buy a new sofa, and if you didn't like it, just say, "You're not letting me be me!"

Vera: That's a ridiculous comparison. We can be alone anytime. We'd be stuck with the sofa.

Marcus: You're missing the point. It just feels respectful to have asked me first, and it hurts that you didn't.

Vera: *You* are missing the point. I want to live my life engaged with the world. I loved getting to be so free and easy. I feel sad that you are making a big deal out of welcoming a new neigh-bor. I wish you could see how controlled I feel by your "rules."

This couple entered treatment having battled for more than a year about this incident and its larger meaning. While there might be many ways they could compromise around freedom and mutuality, the key to unraveling such gridlock is genuine interest in the other's reality. This flash card can get the ball rolling, making "compromise," in fact, unnecessary. Common sense and kindness usually create much more satisfying solutions.

PART VIII

Loving

A spiritual teacher I've learned a great deal from, Saniel Bonder (author of *Great Relief* and *Healing the Mind/Matter Split* [Mt. Tam Empowerments]), makes an excellent point: Don't expect Relationship to give you what only Identity can . . . and don't expect Identity to give you what only Relationship can. What he's saying, in layman's terms, is that there's a place in your soul where only your True Self will ever fill you, but . . . it is not the whole enchilada!

As you may already have figured out for yourself, anyone who believes "there is no such thing as 'having a relationship' with another person . . . there is only being connected to your own insides in that other person's force field," has probably done her time in the Identity camp. In my twenties I had some very powerful spiritual experiences that showed me both that love is a Universal—not just a one-on-one—thing, and that, unbelievably, I can feel whole without another's approval. I discovered I could feel love for a stranger or for someone "creepy." While it's a longer story, I ended up giving up a career in journalism following an incident where an idealized editor told me I had written something "incredibly mediocre," and in the post-meditation space I was in, miraculously, I felt no diminishment.

I promptly spent three decades trying to find a way to sustain the Identity in me that allowed that to happen.

So while this entire book is about making your True Identity matter *in* relationship, I am also here to tell you: Love is all it's cracked up to be. There are times when nothing else will do but loving your partner and, in the case of this book, letting them know that they are, indeed, loved by you. Often we worry about whether our love is "real" or whether we really know how to do it. And there *is* always the danger that a poorly timed expression of our love in the heat of conflict will be labeled by our partner as insincere. But find the courage to make love matter in the midst of a rupture by using one of the following cards, and I promise that it will speak volumes . . . without you having to utter a word.

83.

Right now, I'd do
anything for you to
know how much
I love you.

If you and your partner are in the midst of an unpleasant interaction, it would not be good thinking to present this flash card in the hope that it would magically bring you to a fairy-tale ending. Knowing that your partner adores you won't always make up for the fact that they clearly agreed to go with you to a friend's photography exhibit tomorrow tonight, and now seem to have neither a recollection of this agreement nor an inkling of a desire to go.

"I told you I think it's fantastic that Elaine is starting to exhibit her stuff," your partner says, "but I never said I would go to the opening. I hate that scene, and she's *your* friend. I can see the photographs by myself next week."

"But it's about accompanying *me*, so we can actually do *something* other than watch movies together. You told me you'd come with me . . . I'm not making this up."

"No," your partner says. "I said I'd take a look at the photographs *some*time . . . and you *wanted it* to be tomorrow night . . ." And now the two of you really get into it—you feeling you are asking for so little, your partner acting like you are asking for a lot.

And then your partner leaves the room and comes back holding up this flash card. They are not flashing it to shut you up, but to tell you: I know you are disappointed . . . For whatever reason, I cannot budge on this one . . . What really matters is still intact between us . . . Please, let's make our love be bigger than the not-that-important tension between us.

This card was not designed to be a profound declaration of love to a partner who may be doubting it. It was designed to infuse your interchange with a dose of goodwill—to remind you that underneath this current frustration, our relationship is doing well, and this difference between us is a difference, not a tragedy. Now you can even go on being upset about what you were upset about—but you will notice it will be without rancor.

84.

I love you. And
despite how it looks,
I don't want our
relationship to be a fight.

To me, the thrill of receiving this flash card isn't due to the expression of love or even the noble stand for peace—it's the fact that the person on the other side of the net has figured out that what happens to be going on between us in this moment must look mighty unattractive to me.

It's wonderful hearing that your partner wants it to be friendlier between the two of you, but there's something even more wonderful about them seeing your. . . *hmmm, let's say, feistier* side . . . and knowing it's not really how you want it to be either.

This is a very loving flash card—again, not just because your partner is declaring their love, but because they are feeling your distaste and grasping some unspoken sense of the harm this hostility is causing to your higher vision of things. Likely the Sender of this flash card knows that pretty recently they were certainly, at least, *looking like* a fighter, and it will be calming for the Receiver to know that even though things have gotten pretty messy between you, the two of you still share the same vision of how you'd like things, on a good day, conducted between you.

This won't be true for everyone, but many of us grew up hearing parents yelling at each other a lot. Rarely did one of these parents come to us and say, "Honey, I know all this fighting stinks." Having a reactive partner imply that they know fighting is disturbing tells you something very comforting—not that there will never be another fight, but that the fighter part of your partner is only a small, more immature part of a much more developed human being.

85.

You don't have to be miserable to get me to take you seriously. Talk to me like I'm a friend who wants to do right by you.

Though it would have been less catchy, another solid title for this book, covering a couple of crucial bases in its own right, would have been *Talk to Me Like You Imagine I Love You and Want to Do Right by You*. While I debated whether to include something that would suggest your partner was overdramatizing, I offer "You don't have to be miserable to get me to take you seriously" because we do tend to up the ante when we don't trust our needs will be taken seriously.

Harris was preparing for the "what kind of father are you?" lecture from his wife, Mandy, because a work problem meant he had to renege on time with their son. So he presented as desperate. The way she brought her partner, Gayle, the news that the $800 repair estimate might indicate having to buy a whole new refrigerator, one might have thought Leanne was lobbying for a lifesaving drug. Ruth gave her partner, Roy, some excellent feedback—that she wished when he felt let down by her he could sound more disappointed than neglected—but she herself sounded far more maltreated than disappointed when she shared her observations.

Here's the thing about this: often when we present our needs to our partners from a place of distress and drama, we are asking them to manage *our* anxiety about making the request—but this is not the same as just asking straight for what we need: more time for a project, kind listening about an unexpected expense or a psychodynamic between us. I honestly believe that if we were able to trust that—regardless of the unexpected loss of father-son time—we would still be loved, all of the static around our request would feel unnecessary. This flash card not only supports your partner in owning their needs without fanfare, it opens up the possibility of them finding out how much more friend you are than ogre.

86.

I am not

_____, who

hurt you in the past.

I am _____,

who loves you now.

Once I had a forty-nine-year-old woman in my office for couples therapy with her second husband, stating her frustration using somewhat unusual language. "I'm not even that depressed," she said, probably accurately, "but he acts like I'm drowning, and if he gets too close, I'm going to take him down with me." Ten minutes before the session was over, the woman matter-of-factly answered a routine question I asked about her father by letting me know that when she was five, he drowned in a freak family boating accident in which he was able to save my client and her mother but not himself. And she had *no idea* that she was still psychologically reenacting that tragedy.

Our capacity to project past experience onto the present is infinite. In this particular case, her husband was not avoiding her at all. She was keeping him at a distance because of her own deeply rooted, well-earned fears that her need for care could overwhelm another, if not make them disappear. We all do this—think we "see" familiar clues, then protect ourselves, assuming, "Here it goes again . . . I *know* what this means." And so, as in flash card #83, we will experience our partner not wanting to accompany us to the photography exhibit as rejecting us—rather than just not being in the space for an art opening.

This flash card was designed to help your partner see you as you—not as the father who missed all your football games . . . or the ex-wife who conveyed to you that your touch was clumsy . . . or the mother who told you you looked albino without false eyelashes.

At times when you feel grossly misperceived by your partner and aren't sure where it's coming from, feel free to use this card with the word "anyone" in the first blank.

It can only bring light to the situation.

87.

I am not
_____, who
hurt you in the past.
I am _____,
who loves you now.

This, as you see, is a duplicate of #86. We include it because it is assumed that both you and your partner have a number of revivable skeletons in your respective psyches. Feel free to xerox one of these pages if you need more. Feel free to experiment with putting in the name of the kid in kindergarten who told your beloved in the midst of a class project, "That's a stupid idea," and your partner has referred back to this more than once in your life together. Feel free to fill in generically and offer to perfect strangers.

88

I am not

_____, who

left you in the past. I am

_____, who

isn't going anywhere

without you.

The original wording of the last sentence of this flash card was: "I am _____ who isn't going anywhere." But over and over again in an informal poll of people I know who had been left by lovers, I heard things like, "Whenever we'd have an argument, Mike would say emphatically, 'I'm not going anywhere, honey'—so if you put that on your flash card, it won't be comforting at all." But almost everyone liked the thought "I'm not going anywhere *without you*." Understandable.

Maria remembers being on her third date with Edward and trying to tell him that she was feeling overwhelmed and withdrawn in response to all the violence in the movie they had just seen. But before she could get out, "It's not you—it was the movie," Edward burst forth with, "What could have possibly happened watching a movie that would make you want to stop dating me?" Further examination revealed that Edward was having a flashback to his last girlfriend, Lucy, telling him how "distant" she was feeling—right before she left him.

Maria and Edward have now been married for six years and have this message affixed on their refrigerator with a magnet with Lucy and Maria's names in the right places. Sometimes in a spirit of therapeutic playfulness, Maria announces to Edward, "I am leaving you and running away to live with Denzel Washington at Target." The playfulness accompanied by the flash card helps her husband do what we all need help doing—updating Reality so we might actually want to live there.

89.

You are precious. And
you deserve to be
treated that way.

A good rule of thumb: we don't always need to have our needs met, but things tend to work out much more smoothly if they are at least acknowledged. I know there are many exceptions to this rule, but bear with me. To end up embodying self-worth, it's not that we need to be treated well all the time . . . we need to know that we *deserve* to be treated well.

If a good part of the time as children our parents had followed up insensitive behavior with "You didn't deserve that" or "The punishment didn't fit the crime" or "I was carrying on with you with what I should have confronted my own dad about," we would have grown up far less wounded. The problem with being a kid is that if you feel bad—and unkind or insensitive parental behavior, no matter how unintended, makes you *feel* bad—you believe you *are* bad. If, on the other hand, in your child mind you truly believed you were precious and deserved to be treated

that way, I suspect we could pretty much safely dub you a "neurosis-free" adult. Alas, for many of us, this was far from the case.

Embedded in this flash card is the message "I know I've treated you poorly." (And no one, obviously, would send this to anyone if they had already been treating them as precious.) Trust me—*this is the flash card you wish your partner's parents had regularly flashed to your partner.* If they had, your partner might not have turned into the sometimes overly defensive and self-deprecating person they (and pretty much all of us) can sometimes be.

So here are some recommendations: flash this card to your partner whenever you have treated them poorly. Flash this card to your partner when the world has treated them poorly. Flash this card to your partner when they are treating themselves poorly. And if no one else rises to the occasion, flash this card to yourself without any provocation whatsoever.

90.

I love you and can't
stand seeing you
so unhappy.

A lot of good, solid personal-growth thinking of the last twenty years has many of us perhaps a bit too sensitized to "codependence"—to the point that we question any impulse to take responsibility for another's pain.

When I first felt drawn to this message, I have to admit thinking to myself, "Am I subtly fostering codependent thinking? Will the reader assume I am suggesting that they are, God forbid, *responsible* for their partner's unhappiness?"

Let me just say here and now: it's not always pathological to want a loved one to feel a little miserable when you are feeling a little miserable. And it's certainly not crazy to feel the pain of someone you love.

A note of caution: if it was you who contributed to your partner's unhappiness through sub-wholesome behavior, go peruse section IV, "Taking Responsibility," and find a more appropriate flash card than this one. Your maturity will mean more to your partner than your empathy.

This flash card, on the other hand, is for when your partner has done everything possible to convince her teenage son (not yours) to get a summer job, and the kid only says, "There are no jobs out there—get off my back." It's for when your partner is feeling thwarted by their boss, unsupported by a colleague, invaded by a parent, plagued by a migraine and/or in general feeling like the world is too much with them.

Wait, let me rethink what I said above about going to section IV if you are the cause of your loved one's pain. There are certain times when your actions (or lack thereof) and your partner's disappointment around them are mild enough that this card might be appropriate—perhaps being unable to accompany them to their friend's son's Bar Mitzvah. Use this card and both of you may be surprised to discover that disappointing someone and "I love you" can coexist. That's very hopeful news for your relationship.

91.

I know I sounded like a maniac, but my love for you is still and deep.

Once a fairly neurotic client of mine went out and bought me five dozen roses (think: sixty roses) accompanied by an über-appreciative note for filling out a routine insurance form. I did not feel appreciated—I felt a little weird about it all. When I saw him a month later and he reflectively acknowledged how over-the-top his behavior had been and how hard it must have been to be put in the position of having to thank him for such bounty, I felt moved to send him a few dozen roses myself.

Manic-depressive illness is a serious biochemical disorder that causes enormous pain to those who suffer from it, so I want to be clear that this flash card, and the strand of self-deprecating humor in it, is no commentary at all on that particular disorder. The maniacs I am hoping to address are like the one who flipped out because her partner threw in a load of laundry that included colors and whites (and nothing even bled), the one who gave her husband seven items to buy at Staples and flipped out because the packing tape he bought wasn't "easy-tear," and the one who flipped out on the unsuspecting meter maid who was writing a ticket as he and his wife approached their parked car. I only mention the rose incident because of the relief I felt when someone who had been out of control approached me from groundedness.

Demonstrating the self-observation mind-set to your partner that lets them know you *know* you have been acting maniacally will be instantly relieving to your partner. But the key words here are "still" and "deep." They provide a much-needed counterpoint to your maniacal side, and telegraph to your partner not just that you know you were acting like a lunatic, but that you haven't forgotten that the real basis for the connection between you lies in a quieter, subterranean place, not necessarily in the world they just observed you flipping out in.

92.

I love you.

I hate fighting.

Can't we just hug?

Adam called Rosie before leaving work early one Friday evening, discovered that their nine-year-old daughter was going to a slumber party and happily suggested that the two of them have their own grown-up version. Rosie agreed and kidded her husband that when he came home he might find sleeping bags and M&M's on their living room floor.

Forty-five minutes later, when Adam walked in the door, Rosie was on the phone preoccupied with talking their daughter through some homesickness in an effort to get her to stay at the party rather than come home.

"So quickly you forget *our* party," Adam quipped, saying nothing about their child. "No sleeping bags? No M&M's?"

"So quickly you forget you are a parent," snapped Rosie, concerned about their daughter, not in a playful mood, feeling unpartnered and upset that it didn't register in Adam that she had been working hard to keep their evening child-free.

Within minutes, it became unfriendly between them, each convinced that it was the other who "broke the mood." Adam wanted Rosie to see that he had walked in the house wanting to play with her. Rosie wanted Adam to see how it would have made her feel closer to him if he had showed concern about their child. "I would have felt we were together . . . *That* would be foreplay," she insisted. Maybe yes, maybe no. But when you are hovering between intimacy and self-protectiveness, it's hard to get to a handshake, let alone something closer. Let this friendly flash card pierce that self-protectiveness and take you where you really want to go—not necessarily to bed, but certainly back in your hearts.

.93.

I treasure you.

No field notes or, for that matter, book of poetry could do justice to what might impel you to use this flash card or what it might evoke in your partner. Even "follow your heart" feels like too much advice.

PART IX

Making Up

Any flash card in this book could potentially move you and your partner on the road toward making up. The mere fact of offering anything of a mood-changing nature during an argument—and with all due respect to the flash cards in this book, a white flag might do perfectly fine—can serve to lower defenses and allow everyone in the room to relax a little. Even you couples out there who fight a lot (and you are definitely not alone, there are *a lot* of you out there)—do you ever really get tired of the making-up part? Not really. Particularly if it is truly making up—and not just making nice.

Marital researcher extraordinaire John Gottman, whom I have referred to in a few of the field notes in this book, reports that the happiest couples also fight, and sometimes frequently. The trick to staying happy, according to Gottman, is that you need about four or five more friendly interactions in a day than unfriendly ones. The flash cards in this section are specifically designed to bring sparring or disconnected partners into a friendlier homestretch.

While many of the flash cards in this book—particularly section IV, "Taking Responsibility," and VII, "Apologizing"—have the capacity to melt the Receiver and move the two of you into a full-blown Make Up, the messages in this section were designed to focus on what might be holdbacks to getting there. Some of them are direct requests to move forward together into something warmer.

May you and your partner never lose the joy in making up. Whenever tension and hostility arise, may you get better and better at bringing this specific tenderness into your relationship. That joy and tenderness has a lot to do with finding out that the beloved you feared had disappeared on you actually never left. Making up is a form of reunion, and it is the hope of this book to make these reunions tender, educational and increasingly natural.

94.

I can see how upset you are, and I feel terrible.

These are very ordinary words. They could have come from the mouth of someone who lived a hundred years ago, before anyone knew what the heck "conscious communication" even was. The speaker might be at a loss as to what to say or do after flashing this card—but no matter: they have told you they are aware of your suffering and that it pains them. More often than you'd expect, *this is all you need*.

Fourteen seconds before holding up this card, the Sender could have been attacking you or, conversely, defending themselves, or even just ignoring you. Does it make a difference? Whatever they were doing, they were making it about themselves—their image, their agenda, their holiest intentions, their God-given unalienable needs, the principles without which they cannot be in a relationship. But now . . . they are getting themselves out of the way and just seeing you—and seeing you accurately. *Particularly* if the Sender was previously stuck in their position, the meta-message of this flash card is: nothing matters more to me right now than my beloved feeling better. This is irresistibly free of anyone trying to win anyone over.

Notice how there is no obvious "Taking Responsibility" here. No one is "Apologizing." Yet I'd bet that whatever had been previously upsetting didn't really matter as much as that you didn't feel felt. It doesn't matter that this flash card is generic. You *thought* you wanted to make a specific point, but now you see that all you really wanted was for your partner to feel you. When there's heart in it, how extraordinary the ordinary can really be.

95.

It would mean a lot if you could just say, "I'm sorry." Or do or say something that shows me that you care about what happened.

Perhaps more than other flash cards in the deck, this one requires a fair amount of self-worth and courage to hold up. Be willing to flash it. Because you wouldn't be driven to flash it to your partner if they weren't already showing some signs of being withholding, uncaring, frozen somewhere between guilt and denial, isolating or otherwise insensitive to their impact on you. Which means, frankly, there is a possibility here that you still won't get through—at least not right away.

After calling a friend in Chicago, where he thought his wife was staying for a supposed business meeting, Derek followed the trail and found out that his wife, Cathy, had, in fact, just taken twenty-four hours off from Skokie to go shopping and to the movies and lunch with a girlfriend—nothing Derek would have minded if his wife had only told him the truth.

Following a nanosecond of humiliation, Cathy went into an all-out defense, touching upon: Derek's dependency, her lack of freedom and need for space, evidence why she "knew" he'd never grant her "a simple day to myself" and a litany of hard-to-hear observations on how not-fun Derek was. Nothing she said addressed Derek's suffering after finding out his wife had lied.

Derek was fearful of offering this flash card directly, but when he awoke in the morning, he placed this message on the bathroom mirror and immediately felt lighter. He got nothing from Cathy before he went to work, and no e-mail during the day. But the flash card "worked" from the point of view that Derek stayed connected to the awareness that he *deserved* a caring response; he made the decision not to speak to Cathy until she had something real to give him. The flash card maneuver was a form of throwing down the gauntlet, keeping Derek more interested in aligning with his self-worth than with Cathy—inviting her eventually to give him the sincere apology he had coming to him.

96.

I'm worried that there's no space to make it better between us.

With half of all marriages ending in divorce and a good many of the remaining ones looking lackluster to miserable . . . and with so many other relationships at tense standstills, how could I possibly be thinking that acknowledging how hopeless something seems could do much?

But I am thinking something . . . and that is drawing your partner's attention not to "hopeless," but to "no space." Because I'm guessing that it's not so hopeless that they might not be completely out of touch with the possibility that they are so invested in making you wrong, that at least right now, you have no place to go. So without attack or the slightest criticism, we're putting the ball in their court. If the Receiver has even a drop of goodwill toward you, this flash card will have them a little uneasy as to why, in fact, they haven't been willing to give it to you.

Early in my training I treated a couple who seemed to genuinely like each other, and they both felt pretty terrible about the fact that he would drink heavily and occasionally slug her. And I was shocked when I somehow got the husband to clean up his act, and the wife became suicidal. My initial understanding of this development was that, an abused child herself, the wife felt the absence of abuse as the absence of love. But because of the abuse, she also felt she must be a bad person, and as long as she could see her husband as the bad one, she could feel *she* was good. No longer able to demonize him, the merest tension triggered her own worst feelings about herself.

This is often what is going on when it feels like there's no space to make it better. Your partner and the relationship get stranded in the heartbreakingly human endeavor of clutching for one's own goodness. Flash this message and silently beam to your partner, "I know you are good." And you will know you both are.

97.

We need a new
perspective. Let's take a
break and each get
clearer about what really
matters here. Okay?

Confucius said, "The way out is through the door . . . oh, why is it that no one will use this method?" Okay, it's not a perfect analogy, but a pretty good one: Why is it that couples locked in a painful interaction rarely use a little common sense and take a short time-out to regroup? While we are at it, we might also ask, Why would a child throw a tantrum in the supermarket instead of calmly negotiating for the gummy bears he so desires? Why would a teenager take money off your dresser without first asking? Why are they fighting in the Middle East? You get the picture: there are some things that are just beyond us humans. When we feel our needs won't be met—real or imagined needs, I should add—we can go into a self-protective, combative trance. Many trances go on for decades, a few for centuries. This flash card can help you get out of the (I hope) short-term trance you might be in with your beloved.

Of course, whichever one of you retrieves this flash card in the first place is already starting to wake up. Let's say it's you. You are telling your partner a lot—that you have faith that there's an answer not yet hit upon, and that what really matters to them could well hold a clue to this treasure. (This will soften their resistance to giving up their current treasure—their grievance against you.) You are acknowledging that they are human and *deserve* a little break. And the *"Okay?"* is more than cosmetic. Instead of attempting to rip them away from the project they have been invested in for the last two and a half hours—debating you—you are offering an invitation they are free to decline.

Only they won't. Because you are finally sounding so sensible to them. Because you are approaching them as a real partner in this. Because they know whatever impelled you to regroup was kind. Because, unlike how you were five minutes ago, you sound mature.

98.

I would love it if we could just be quiet and hold each other.

This is what this card is *not* to be used for: to get your partner to stop talking about something that matters to them but is making you uncomfortable . . . to avoid talking about or taking responsibility for something that ought to matter *to you* . . . to move your partner into a sexual situation under the guise of suggesting friendly, healing contact. Even as I write this, I regret introducing any suspiciousness into this field note, but I am doing so because I want to preserve the sanctity of this flash card. That's how potentially beautiful it is.

There's a certain point in a rupture with your partner where you are kind of spent, you notice you might be listlessly repeating yourself because you've gotten your essential points out, something doesn't seem so life-and-death anymore, your partner seems more reasonable than they appeared fifteen minutes ago and, frankly, you are not sure where to go next. It's no longer combative, but it's not exactly cozy either. I say, go for it . . . go for cozy. Look, I'm a wordsmith—this whole book is about using words to bridge the gaps between human beings. But even I know that often it is the nonverbal connection between you that is what is going to feel really, really real—when you can stop thinking and move into the gentleness that makes you wonder how things could have possibly gotten so nutty between you.

Holding each other, by the way, does not have to be in a horizontal position. You might be in a place where standing in a sustained hug is what most honors the moment. Or one of you might sit on the other's lap. One couple I know finds it calming to sit on the floor back-to-back in silence, and then speak from that place.

An upset does not have to be 100 percent resolved to offer this flash card. But feel into it—it can be a tender, if not inspired, way to take a magic carpet ride from third base to home.

99.

I feel really crummy
about what happened.
Could we just make up?

think of this flash card as "no frills." But receiving it can be quite thrilling. It is rare that someone does not like knowing that their partner feels crummy about the argument they've just had.

If you are the one who usually tends to process an upset with passion before getting to the finish line, your less-process-oriented partner will be thrilled—not to mention down-on-their-knees grateful—that you were willing to offer this card and go straight to the making-up module. And in the rarer, but not unheard of, situation where the less communicative one of you initiates sending this flash card, you, who thrives on thoroughly getting to the bottom of an interaction, will be compensated for your loss by knowing that your partner did something so elegantly proactive in the relating sphere.

Any reluctance to use this card is usually around "Are we moving to closure too soon?" But think of it this way: since most of your processing of an upset is an attempt to get your partner to feel crummy about what just happened, why not just try going there first? You may say to me, "But if I'm the one to flash this card, how do I *know* my partner is feeling crummy?" The answer is, you don't. But think about it, sweetheart. Can you *really* imagine your partner saying anything other than, "Me too"?

100.

I want to hug you, and I'm not sure I am welcome. May I come closer?

You might read this flash card and think, "What has this world come to? You need a written request to get a hug? Gimme a break!"

Well, I say—give yourself a break. All you have to do is think of all the times you went to hug someone at the end of a fight, and the moment you touched them, you knew they weren't really with you yet. And think of all the times *you* were willing to hug someone without really being present with them, but wanting to show you were a good sport. It wasn't satisfying.

I've spent lot of time thinking about this flash card, and I want to be clear that it's really not about negotiating for a hug. It's more a kind of litmus test you can perform to get a better read on where your partner is with you. Sometimes the two of you have genuinely resolved something between you, but you were so physiologically activated and upset prior, that one or both of you may not have fully returned to your body. If you flash this to your partner and they say, "I don't think I'm there yet, but I appreciate that you asked first," I'd consider this a sweet move in the right direction. You have had one small friendly, boundaried interaction that went well. Bravo!

If your partner is on the border between no-hug and hug, this card will probably move them over the line. If your partner nods their head yes, and is sincere about it, the fact that you were so respectful of their boundaries will make the hug more meaningful. If your partner shakes their head no, then thank them for telling you the truth and not going through the motions. In other words, let this be a bid for connection on your part where you stay connected to your heart, regardless of whether your partner is ready to hug you or not.

I am willing to bet that the vulnerability in this flash card will evoke something honest in the Receiver. It might not be a hugging partner who is suddenly meeting you halfway . . . but it will be one who appreciates that you gave them the opportunity to kindly speak their truth.

IOI.

I forgive you completely.
It never happened.

For many years, this flash card just read, "*I forgive you. Completely.*" And "completely" certainly covers a wide expanse of time, space and memory. But as time went on, I came to see that "completely" isn't necessarily foolproof. It's amazing how seemingly forgiven and forgotten grievances can pop right back into your head again when it feels like your partner is being perverse, irresponsible, spaced out or hitting below the belt. Or when their post-forgiveness behavior or energy veers even slightly in the direction of the original crime.

That's partially because when you forgave them the first time, you didn't make it to "It never happened." What could I possibly mean? How could I—who have been exhorting you all along to be in Reality—suggest that when your partner allowed your health insurance to lapse for three weeks . . . when they carried on like a madperson with the neighbor who used the "wrong" pesticide . . . when they mindlessly left your four-year-

old's birthday party to help their secretary with a home repair . . . how could I encourage "It never happened"?

Stay open, okay? I am asking you to try on the idea that anything your partner did that was that offensive was simply *not done in their right mind*. (Actually, if you think of the examples above, might you not say to your partner, "Are you *out of your mind* allowing us to go without insurance?") The real them— the one you love and trust—was not, I promise you, running the show when they did what they did. It was their workaholic or rage-aholic or codependent sub-self. The real them would *never* have behaved so horribly. And you know this, even as you argue, "So what if the real them played hooky!"

No one is holding a gun to your head to forgive your partner—and you may not be ready—but if you genuinely want to forgive your partner and let go of your resentment, this is the ticket. You are not offering this flash card to let your partner off the hook.

You are offering it to remind yourself that what is unblemished in your partner is still intact and that they are still a worthy recipient of your finest love. You are reminding yourself that the Good in life is more real than the Not Good. You are reminding yourself of how you want to be treated when it is you who happens to be not in your right mind.

PART X

Making

Love

Sex is supposed to be one of the most naturally pleasurable things in the world, and yet it is amazing just how quickly an interpersonal disconnect can turn "natural" into strategic and "pleasurable" into awkward, anxiety-ridden and . . . something one would be happy just to avoid altogether.

I've experienced several dozen men in my practice who have been in ten- or fifteen-, even twenty-year trances in which they are unable to get over the fact that the woman who enthusiastically made love with them during their courtship days seems to have long ago transmuted into someone who (as they perceive it) thinks about sex about as often as they savor their tenth-grade earth science notes. "She liked it . . . she loved it . . . I know she did!" These men are close to tears wanting to convince me that they were not hallucinating.

So here's the thing. The men aren't making it up. It's just that there's a serious gap between the woman they're fantasizing about and the one they're actually living with. This is because after the head-over-heels hormones recede in women, it's Presence that, for the most part, turns them on. Women don't stop thinking about sex. They are thinking about it all the time, but their thoughts can become more along the lines of "He's going to want to have sex later . . ." or "I haven't been giving him much attention all week (or he seems to be stressed out). I better make love tonight" or "I'd love him to give me a back rub, but I know he's going to turn it into foreplay . . . For once, could it just be a back rub?!" or "I'd love to really show him how I want to be kissed, but I know he'll just hear it as criticism" or "How can he expect me to want sex when he's been making love to his iPad all week?" Meanwhile, men spend half their time wanting sex and the other half worrying about how to minimize rejection when it is denied (okay, this is an exaggeration, but you get my point).

That I could suggest taking on such body-mind-spirit complexity with a flash card could seem like chutzpah or gross naïveté, unless you take seriously that something has gotten in the way of "natural" and "pleasurable." The flash cards in this section are meant to target that something—I'd call it some form of worry—that of itself may not be that big a deal, but unaddressed can become one hell of an antiaphrodisiac. It could be worry about anticipated out-of-syncness, the state of one's body, feeling used, feeling controlled, just for starters. But worrying out in the open will have you liking yourself and your partner more. Which is why the best making love flows from first making nice.

102.

I want to make love—but only if you are liking me.

et's just say, you wouldn't flash this card to your partner out of the blue. It is meant to be used when there has been some disconnect, and maybe even some grown-up processing of the disconnect, and, while the Sender is definitely feeling warmer, he or she is still living on that uncertain edge where they fear that making love would demonstrate they've softened—only to find out after the fact that their partner still has "stuff going on." With this card, you're sort of telling your partner: "I love you, I'm ready to be a pal—but not a schmuck . . . Your move."

Wordsmith that I am, I'm curious about how not right it feels to say, "I want us to make love—but only if you are loving me." Why would that be? I'm not sure why, but such a declaration with an intimate partner feels insulting—implying at one end of the spectrum that love can be commanded and, on the other, that it might even have disappeared.

There's a lot of self-respect packed into this flash card. And even taking into account my occasional tendency to exaggerate to make a point, I believe that being deeply aligned with this message is the most concentrated and effective form of sex therapy on the planet.

In my practice, whether a couple is presenting with a humiliation over the fact that she whispered to him at a buffet, "Do you really need potatoes *and* bread?" . . . or they are having a seemingly more neutral discussion about whether their ten-year-old would fare better at a boys' basketball camp or a traditional coed camp . . . the interaction will almost always go better if they *begin* in a friendly space. I can't say this is universal, but for some of you, flashing this card could be high-level foreplay. And I can say that because . . . ? Because it could deeply align your body and heart—a very good place to begin.

103.

I'd love it if we could go slow.

This card wins the "most popular" vote. Of the first ten women to whom I mentioned I was now coming up with "flash cards for real sex," eight suggested some version of it. (A handful of these women actually said the card should simply say: "SLOWER, PLEASE.")

I've given the question of why men seem to enjoy going fast a lot of thought. The obvious conclusion, based on a synthesis of the givens of male physiological arousal and the analysis of some of the greatest thinkers from the Men-Don't-Get-It Hut, is that "Men go too fast because they aren't sensitive enough." But I think something else is going on. Women, by nature and nurture, are geared to be responsive to the needs of others, and the speed issue is confabulated by their great difficulty ignoring what they think the guy wants or the tempo in which he wants it. In other words, maybe we're not being clear enough with men what we want.

Perhaps you have heard of the research coming out of Harvard on girls' development. Take a ten-year-old girl out for pizza, ask her what she wants, and she happily asserts, "Pepperoni!" A twelve-year-old might begin with "I'm not sure . . ." And sadly, too many fourteen-year-old girls respond with "What do *you* want?" We can see this as women needing assertiveness training and boundary-setting boot camp . . . or we can see this as requiring some mutual consciousness where a woman can acknowledge this tendency without shame and her partner is called upon to be mindful of how she can lose herself in sex and everywhere else. What you really want is a partner who is slowing himself down because he appreciates your needs AND your psychological predicament—not because he sees you as a traffic signal. And when you are saying "slow," you may need to add a clarifier or two like "contactful" or "following my pace" . . . or perhaps, "You know, honey . . . dreamy."

104

I want to make love with you, too, but first I need to ask you something— and please don't hate me for asking—have you been avoiding conflict with me all day so that tonight doesn't get derailed?

At first I hesitated to even include this card, as it could so easily be read as questioning a loved one's goodwill and good deeds. So why did I persevere and include it? Because sometimes the awkwardness and possible sting of the moment might be the price you have to pay to have an experience where you aren't going through the motions.

Through years of working with couples, I have learned never to underestimate the human capacity to feel managed, humored or manipulated. And it's these undertones *unaddressed* that can ultimately turn lovemaking into a duty. To the reader squirming at the thought of presenting this card, I want to hold up a flash card that says, "Please, don't hate *me*! I'm on the side of you having the most intimate, juicy relationship possible." If you are honest with yourself, when you are not fully trusting your partner's "connectivity," something gets lost in the togetherness

department. Actually, this flash card epitomizes one of the theories underlying this whole book: that when you are connected in your partner's force field to your own internal stirrings—even conceivably paranoid ones—things just go better.

It's not easy being a lover of a woman. I understand Dr. Phil not long ago started circulating a directive to men that is not without merit: Foreplay begins "twenty-four hours before." *Really?* you might ask. *How is any woman to know whether her man is operating out of devotion or strategy?* To which I'd say: And when you are wondering about your partner's "ulterior motives," think of all the times you might have made love—to use a phrase—just to avoid conflict. Think about that! We men and women are really not that different from each other in terms of navigating the misty areas between strategy and devotion.

105.

When we are out of sync, you act like something is very wrong. Nothing's wrong— we just need to get back in sync . . .

Note: It is recommended that the holding up of this card be accompanied by a hand gesture: arm extended, palm upward, reaching out in what most people would call an "inviting" gesture.

In card #66: *"What can I say that would make you feel understood?"* I talk about a woman who is trying to communicate to her partner that it's frustrating to her that when lovemaking doesn't seem to be going ideally, he quickly concludes that she's "just not that into it," and withdraws. The point I was making had to do with simply dealing with relationship gridlock in general.

Now that we're giving ourselves permission to talk about sex per se, however, I think I have something better to give you. And I'm feeling motivated, because while it is true that there are many times that someone, particularly a female someone, "isn't in the mood," I cannot tell you all the times women have told me they have thrown their hands up because their partners likely sensed some molecule of them not responding in a familiar or desired way . . . that they were not 100 percent present, even momentarily—dare I say it—distracted . . . and it was curtains.

There's a re-emerging body of thought developed by a brilliant psychologist, Silvan Tomkins, in the sixties called Affect Theory. Tomkins concluded that shame was a *reflexive* biological response to "pleasure interrupted" or "interest withdrawn," and if I am understanding the theory correctly, there is no amount of personal growth work that can stop the reflexive shame response to perceived withdrawal from getting triggered— only understood and owned as automatically occurring. If you are not yet with a partner who can tell you in the moment, "Honey, you don't seem to be totally meeting me right now, and I notice my shame response getting activated," be mindful of your partner's likely unconscious diminishment and hold out this card . . . and your hand. And remember that when he broadly assumed you were just not that into it, when for the most you were approaching him with warmth, you probably felt a flash of shame before you got exasperated.

106.

When you give me the message that you think I'm just a guy "looking to get laid," it feels like you don't see me.

It is very hard to grow up in this culture—no, make that, galaxy—without concluding that men think about sex *a lot*. Men, in fact, routinely have to let other men know they share this assumed obsession, to be one of the guys. Young women in their sexually formative years get the message they are torturing their dates by "withholding" sex. You may be expecting me to now say something like "But it isn't true . . . Men are thinking about lots of other things beyond sex." But I'm not going to say that, because men *are* thinking about sex a lot and wanting it a lot—which doesn't mean that they can't fall in love. It takes a lot of self-worth on a woman's part to perceive his—for lack of a better phrase—self-interest, and not presume it's a sure sign his genitals are detached from his heart.

On occasion, one of my clients has handed me a check and I suddenly kiss it, clutch it to my chest, and croon, "I *love* getting paid for what I do!" And then I say to them, "Can you still trust that I deeply care about you?" It is so unexpected that most people are put into a trance. But my goal isn't to make them uncomfortable—it's to get them to see how hard it is to trust another's care when that other is "getting something out of it."

Frankly, it's taken a while for me to escape from the galactic illusion of male self-centeredness myself, but I can say with certainty that it is deeply, deeply wounding for a basically decent guy to get the message that his sexual desire for his partner lacks heart or is evidence that he is using her. Are men sometimes oblivious to women's feelings? Yes. Do men sometimes fantasize about women just tending to them? Yes. But a man who flashes this card is standing up for his humanness and subtly conveying to the woman in front of him her own capacity to objectify another person.

107

I know I behaved badly,
but I don't want to
have sex just to make
it up to you. Can we
clear things first?

One of the trickiest things about help-ing a couple navigate sexual issues in their relationship is avoiding gender stereo-types. I am at least enlightened enough to know that there is always a possibility that, as a woman, I might have a somewhat skewed perception regarding the whole male-female thing. This said, it may happen in some mu-nicipality unknown to me, but I've never heard of a woman upset that her man isn't helping more around the house change her tune because this man kissed her the right way. Or, for that matter, of a quickie—no matter how good—silencing a female party who is sick and tired of her man spending too much time at the office. Not in my township.

So for the woman (or man) who might be inclined to participate in "makeup sex" be-fore they really feel made up, this card was created to support your courageous commit-ment to engage with your partner cleanly and maturely. Sex as penance will leave you with one more thing to feel guilty about—having betrayed yourself. And if that's not enough to feel lousy about: it certainly won't help your relationship to reinforce the idea that your partner needs to be appeased, not re-lated to.

108.

I'm making up right now that you are feeling sexually deprived. My pattern is to make love to keep you from being upset with me. Let's do it differently this time.

There's some crossover between this card and the one before it (#107: *"I know I behaved badly, but I don't want to just have sex to make it up to you . . ."*), one difference being that the Sender didn't actively screw up, as in charging $750 worth of new clothing on your debit card, causing the $500 check given to your nephew as a wedding gift to, embarrassingly, bounce.

But this is more subtle and endemic. One partner—typically, but not always, the man—seems to be feeling unattended to, unrelated to or just plain sexually frustrated. Theoretically, these feelings could run the gamut from being totally appropriate, healthy and reality-based to insecurity-driven, neurotic and compulsive. Only we should add that it is rare in an ongoing intimate relationship that the entity called "just plain sexually frustrated" ever arises as "just plain . . ." There can be such a groundswell of feelings of hurt (*"How can you be so oblivious to what I have been wanting?"*) and shame (*"I feel like a beggar . . ."*) that the person cast as the Depriver feels extremely called upon to be responsive to the irritability that is protecting her partner from feeling the more vulnerable feelings associated with an alleged sexual lapse.

So the Sender of this card is someone who wants to give up using sex to protect herself from being seen as an Ice Queen. And hopefully encourage her partner to give up using irritability as a way of masking his underlying vulnerability. If you want my opinion, I think these two should talk. And the use of this flash card would not only be a momentous icebreaker in the individual User's relationship—but a transformational moment in the history of Human Relationships. What would making love be like if *neither of you* were using sex as a medication—meaning, as a way of avoiding unspoken, uncomfortable feelings? Wow.

109

I know you like
to verbally process
what's going on in our
relationship first—but
right now, if we could
just touch each other, it
could help me be more
present with you.

Anyone who's gotten this far in this book surely surmises I'm a big fan of communication. So I'm aware that for many of my readers, the inclusion of this flash card may come as a surprise. Not process first? What kind of craziness is she getting into?

I *am* a big fan of communication and, like many of my gender, communicating with you helps me feel safe. However, I'm also an equal opportunity employer . . . And I know that for many people—typically, but definitely not always, males—touching and being touched is what produces a feeling of safety. So let's keep this simple, as God intended it: This is not a flash card encouraging or even supporting sexual contact between two alienated partners who are hoping for a non-verbal miracle. It is, however, for a somewhat triggered, somewhat shut down or somewhat worried friend of yours who is asking for some palpable reassurance that will allow him or her to feel safer in your company.

And remember, ladies, someone wanting to touch "first" before talking isn't inherently valuing your body over "you" or avoiding the fact that you might be pretty upset. Be careful that you don't allow your own need to connect in your preferred modality to become so dominant that you are unable to honor the way that your partner might need first "to process" what has been going on between you before making love.

110.

I would love to share
a sexual fantasy I have
with you and I want
it to bring us closer.

This card is for the thousands upon thousands of people who find it challenging to share with their partner what turns them on—even if they don't want to actually do what they want to "talk" about. A trick for the somewhat inhibited: the parameters in terms of "sexual fantasy" don't have to be so strict. For example, you might tell your partner a not-particularly-sexual fantasy you have about wanting to live with the Aborigines and never again have to make money, wear clothes, mow the lawn or attend a PTA meeting. Yet even this fairly tame fantasy can be shared in a way that could trigger PTSD in your partner, or you can turn it into a moment where you have their curiosity and they are simply getting to know you better. Sharing your stuff—sexual or otherwise—with the latter energy is the ticket. It optimizes the possibility that your partner will want to help make into realities any fantasies you actually do want to come true . . .

III

It's true. I'm not in a space to be sexual right now. Still, I love you and don't want you to make more of it than it really is (i.e., like this is the beginning of the end!) . . . Okay?

This is a case where you'd think the message could and should be easy to verbalize. Even the most conservative estimate of how many times this sentiment was expressed in households across America in the past week would be about a kabillion. Still, it is the rare person who can communicate "not being in the space" without a dose of defensiveness thrown in the mix.

When one person wants to make love and the other doesn't, there is often the normal sting of simply finding out that your happy assumption that your partner is in the same amorous state you are . . . just isn't the case. (Feel into it—aside from any sexual or contact frustration, it can just feel a little embarrassing when you just assumed your partner would want what you were wanting.)

It's also hard being the one not in the mood without at least a trace of feeling like a Depriver—a condition that inspires all sorts of not-really-necessary justifications for not being in the mood ("Do you have any idea what it was like being at the office today with Agnes on maternity leave?" "Have you forgotten all the hours I put in finding a new urologist for your mother?" "I've schlepped the kids all day . . . *and now this*?" etc., etc.).

Take the time to locate and flash this card. The effort involved will show care for your partner's disappointment, vulnerability and fear that this is a portent that something has "changed" between you—and there will be more lean times ahead. This card will keep you from justifying your unavailability. It's just kind.

112.

I'm terrified of pressuring you, but I'm worried that if we keep ignoring that we haven't made love in forever, we'll be past the point of no return. Talk to me about it . . . That's all I ask.

Much has been written about sexless marriages in the last few years—and if what I am hearing from my clients is any indication, it's all true. This is not an easy problem, because it is almost always compounded by a let's-not-talk-about-it pact. Typically, though, one pact maker is far less happy with the arrangement than the other. No magical, sensual promises here—but this could be a situation where the surprise sincerity and boldness of a written flash card could at least create what psychologists call "pattern interruption."

Bear with me while I give you a new way of thinking about interrupting the pattern. Many years ago, my husband of record and I attended a workshop for therapists dealing with sex. The presenter, David Schnarch, Ph.D., author of *Passionate Marriage: Keeping Love and Intimacy Alive in Committed Relationships*, said, "We are now going to begin sex therapy. Please hold your partner's hand." And then not a word for what seemed like a very long time. He then said, "Please let go of your partner's hand." And then he asked us to each go over every second of the encounter, rigorously scanning for any moments of anxiety throughout the entire exercise: when he first announced the task . . . finding a comfortable position for elbows . . . making eye contact or not . . . feeling envious of the couple next door making goo-goo eyes . . . feeling bored or worrying that your partner felt bored . . . feeling either "dropped" or "detained" when he called it a day.

Then he said, "Okay, now we *really* start sex therapy. Tell your partner every molecule of your anxiety. *And then notice when you felt closer—holding hands or talking about your anxiety?*"

I appreciate that for the frustrated partner in a sex-deprived marriage, more talk isn't what you are hankering for. But if a room full of pseudoliberated, moderately in-touch shrinks discovered they were operating in a sea of undisclosed anxiety that was impeding flow—starting to talk anxiety-talk with your partner could become the foreplay to foreplay.

113.

I'm thinking that you're thinking that I should know what you are wanting right now. I wish I did, honey, but I don't.

Sherry, a pretty tuned-in client of mine, reports the following incident: One night she and her husband, Jason, were watching a movie in bed around 10:00 p.m., and both of them were having trouble keeping their eyes open, until Jason finally said, "Sweetie, let's go to bed." They snuggled for a few minutes and Sherry rolled over to go to sleep. Ten minutes later, she says, she could feel Jason's restlessness and so she turned around and said, "You okay, honey?" Sounding somewhere between upset and confused, Jason looked straight ahead, and as if he were having an existential conversation with God, wondered aloud, *Why aren't we making love?* She resisted giving him a hostile retort on the order of "Because we don't do necrophilia"—because he seemed genuinely distressed. This is how the conversation continued:

Sherry: I honestly thought we were both too tired for sex.

Jason: I *was* tired, but not too tired to make love.

Sherry (now mildly irritated): Well, look—you have to help me here. It's up to you to tell me, "I may look tired, but guess what—not below the waist."

Jason: Why should I have to tell you . . . why didn't you just *know?*

I'm not creative enough to make this up. And, point taken: Sometimes when a partner "just knows" and takes loving action, we can feel *very* taken care of—cherished. This is precisely how we know love in the beginning of life when we haven't learned to speak yet and our caregivers better be a little psychic. But hear this in print: this is NOT the norm, nor should it be amongst adults. You should not be expected to read your partner's mind—in fact, this expectation will keep both of you perpetually unrelaxed. But knowing that sometimes your partner *wishes you could*—that could be a very loving thing.

114.

I'm out of words,
and maybe even you
are, too. Please,
just be with me.

Fear not. We won't be adding too much more talk. Simply flash card . . . Smile from heart . . . Open both arms wide . . .

PART XI

Deepening Trust

A friend and mentor of mine, Ted Strauss, is a hard-core metaphysician—meaning he has a profound interest in comprehending whatever is comprehensible about how the Universe works. He is able to write in a nuanced way about divine intelligence, human relationships, quantum physics and existential suffering and interweave these vast subject areas only as one who sees the Bigger Picture can; his essays have titles like "The Self You Didn't Want to Realize," "The Pain of Unity," "The Secret of the Awakening Process" and "Will Consciousness Make you Happy?" I make the case for the complexity of his worldview to highlight the stark simplicity of his essay entitled "Trust," which I will now give you in its entirety:

Trust is everything.

It is, and theoretically, like Ted, I could stop here, except you reading this deserve some bridge between the self-trust inherent in offering a flash card and the creation of the mutual trust that will allow you more and more to relax in your relationship . . . which, by the way, if you really think about it, is why you bought this book in the first place. You can relax with your partner if you can easily be yourself with him or her . . . and you can relax with your partner if you can trust that they are being themselves—both transparent and forthcoming— with you. At the risk of oversimplifying the "everything" alluded to above, this, to me, would pretty much cover "trust." The flash cards in this section were designed to go the next step in specifically addressing those aspects of your relationship where you cannot relax because trust is missing. This is where: I'm afraid you won't see my good intentions . . . where you won't have the shock absorbers to hear my distrust . . . where I'll have to pretend I trust you or feel more understood than I really do . . . where I'm getting an inkling of my own untrustworthi- ness, and how that might feel in your skin . . . where I'm afraid I can never get to be just human with you.

This is the advanced class, and for what it's worth, I've never seen a relationship that I'd call rock solid that didn't eventually have to take this senior honors seminar: acknowledging to each other—our soul mate connection aside—some of the places where, well, we don't fully trust each other. It's a high level of trust to confide one's distrust—and much more honoring of the relationship than either idealizing your partner or treating them as untrustworthy. It can be awkward, but it's one of the most exquisite ways you can teach yourself that permitting your distrust will deepen your beloved's trust of you. And the flash card will help you be kind about it.

115.

I want to hear
what's upsetting you—
but you need to start
slow . . . Okay?

Between the first edition of this book and the one you are reading, John Gottman, Ph.D., previously mentioned relationship analyst extraordinaire, came out with his masterwork, *The Science of Trust*. The following take-away from the book is quite relevant to our flash card in this instance: In the happiest relationships, a woman feels that when she's upset, her partner is taking her distress seriously—not focusing on feeling criticized, shamed, controlled, unappreciated or otherwise treated unfairly (and people wonder why over 51 percent of all marriages end in divorce?).

Gottman fortunately doesn't just leave us with the idea that if women could simply let it out and men could only listen better, we'd be all set. He tells us *how* this Upset But Potentially Happy Person might share her grievances if she actually wants to deepen trust in her relationship. She needs to begin with what's called "a slow start-up." If she begins harshly or sharply (e.g., "I can't believe you even believe such horseshit!!" or "You forgot . . . *again*?!!"), her partner will become so self-protective that his basic flooding mechanism will come into play, and for the moment, anyway, all the apologies in the world—and flash cards (sigh)—will not be able to put Humpty Dumpty together again. Of course, for a woman to quickly convert her grievance into something listener-friendly, she has to locate enough pre-existing trust in herself and her partner's basic goodness to forestall a make-sure-he-gets-it frontal attack. And the man who has the consciousness to choose this card and request sensitivity, rather than go with his instinctive avoidance button, is already demonstrating an inordinate amount of faith in his partner. There are definitely certain situations where trust has to be earned. But there's something beautiful about when it's just given at the get-go. And when it is, well, just sit back and enjoy watching the trust deepen.

116.

I know I was off—but I'm worried you would rather clobber me than get close again.

There's an ongoing background conversation in the world of couples therapy around the issue of "safety." Everyone agrees that it's important to feel safe with your partner, but there are different ideas about where that safety is supposed to come from. The view of one camp of therapists could best be summed up by quoting the following words from a famous therapist who nonchalantly asked our group, "Anyone here wish their partner were more relaxed, more intimate or more fun?" Of course, everyone raised their hand, to which the therapist quipped, "Well, then, *ask yourself: What can you do to make your partner feel safer with you?*" No one expected him to say this, and for the moment, at least, it felt great considering that more relaxation, intimacy and fun could actually be in one's own hands, independent of the rigidities of one's impossible significant other.

A therapist from a quasi-opposing camp would argue that, in the end, no one can "make it safe" for you—it's an inside job. The idea here is that you need to trust your own reality enough to say the candid but potentially provocative thing, and when you imagine, say, your partner rolling their eyes in exasperation or instantly becoming offended that you could even entertain such a thought about them, your job is to automatically comfort and protect your frightened inner child and feel good that the Adult You is being so real and forthright.

I'd say that both approaches have their merits, neither stands alone, and that sharing the responsibility of co-creating safety for each other and oneself is an essential task of transforming a so-so relationship into a wonderful one. This flash card epitomizes taking responsibility for one's own safety . . . by smartly inviting your partner to participate in the process. And as always, an approach acknowledging that you weren't Ms. or Mr. Perfection demonstrates not only that you want closeness—but that you can understand why your beloved might *want to* clobber you . . . just a bit.

117.

I'm not going to clobber you. I only want to repair this with you.

think it's just about a truism that when we've genuinely provoked someone we usually *end up* feeling (if such things could be measured) at least as guilty, if not more so, than our "victim" feels retaliatory.

For instance: Nora had had an issue with Damon being characteristically "too helpful" with other women—like helping a recent divorcée in their neighborhood with home repairs when their own home was in tatters, always enthusiastically offering to get drinks for women at parties and, in Nora's opinion, grossly overtipping waitresses. They focused on this issue in therapy and Damon quickly made the connection between this behavior and the fact his father died when he was ten and his mother quickly instated him as man of the house. Damon truly had taken himself on in correcting these boundary incursions. Still, a few months passed and Nora freaked out because Damon was spending excessive time at a neighbor's—only she freaked out before she had time to find out that Damon had run over the woman's cat and was in a state of total misery, apologizing and appropriately comforting the bereft pet owner.

Now Nora was in a state of horrified guilt—that not only hadn't she given her husband support when he was feeling horrible, but she thought the worst of him when he was handling the situation maturely. This is a situation where a part of Nora believed she was such a bad wife and terrible friend that she deserved to be clobbered. This is an excellent time to use this flash card—when you know you've been treated unkindly and you make the choice to remember that your perpetrator is actually feeling worse than you are . . .

118.

My need for you to see
my good intentions was
so overpowering, I acted
like you didn't exist.
I feel terrible.

When I was in third grade I had a painful incident. I was in Hebrew school, and for the first time in my life wasn't one of the brighter kids in the class. In fact, I felt like the dumbest. My Hebrew teacher was an intimidating Israeli who talked incessantly about fighting Arabs, which I could have tolerated if he had just ignored me. But he was a hostile guy who frequently picked on the slower learners, ridiculing us and mimicking our poor pronunciation. One day "Mr. Solomon" reported that all the water was turned off in the synagogue and he seemed genuinely upset that a potted plant of his in our classroom would die without immediate first aid. I excused myself and returned with a small pitcher of water, absolutely expecting to save the day and win over Mr. Solomon's heart for eternity.

"Where did you get the water, Chana?" Mr. Solomon asked, calling me by my Hebrew name. "From the toilet bowl!" I happily exclaimed, assuming he'd be bowled over by my cleverness. And true to form, Mr. Solo-mon made a disgusted look and told the class, "Knowing where Chana got the water, I would prefer my plants to die."

The combination of my desire to be seen as good and helpful going unrecognized with the implication I had done something dirty (not to mention that one doesn't need a doctorate in psychology to guess that my desire for approval from a father figure might well have come into play) was too much to bear. It was my last day in Hebrew school and pretty much the end of my relationship with organized religion.

Fast-forward to a year ago. My partner, Tim, and I were having a disagreement over how he handled something, and I was pretty sure I was right. But not so sure that I didn't ask a friend of ours, Janice, what she thought of the matter. (To be completely honest, I was figuring that Janice would agree with me.) Lo and behold, Janice pointed out a blind spot of mine, and totally aligned with Tim's manner of handling things. I saw the light, felt humbled and made a beeline for

Tim, anxious to correct my distorted view of things and give him the apology I now saw he deserved.

"YOU SHARED *THAT* WITH JANICE!?" He was infuriated and incredulous. "That was *private!*" (Fear not, dear Reader, we now have Tim's permission to share this much of this incident.) I felt crushed and disoriented and triggered. If you take my history into account, you can understand how disappointing it was for me that he didn't immediately burst forth with, "Oh, Nancy, I love that you were willing to go to the ends of the earth to find the truth of the matter and give me such a sweet and sincere apology. I'm so blessed to have a woman with so much integrity in my life." *But I'm not the only one here with a history.* I am with a man who has a history of having his boundaries repeatedly disrespected, and so the filter through which he heard me come to Jesus wasn't that I was seeing the light and,

in fact, finally seeing his wise perspective . . . *but that I wasn't seeing his vulnerability at all and so I wasn't, in fact, seeing him.*

So who is "right" here? Tim? Me? Everyone has a history and everyone has a perspective.

I share this story—with Tim's blessing—because this is moving us into the advanced class in creating trust. I can virtually promise you that some of the biggest fights you and your partner have ever had are the result of one or both of you not feeling the other is seeing your Goodness in the matter. You may never give up wanting your partner to see your Goodness—nor, perhaps, should you—*but you can give up being addicted to your partner seeing your Goodness.* This is the trick—trust in your own Goodness, and remember your partner needs to feel *he or she exists* more than you need a gold star. This is your Goodness in action. And trust me . . . you'll get seen.

119.

I need you to give
me some space
to be human.

My guess is that many women, in particular, who are reading this book have a sense of their own growth trajectory somewhere along the lines of "the old me," who was too nice or too willing to make nice, too approval-seeking and basically too afraid to make waves or have someone irritated with them . . . and "the new me," who would rather be real than "nice," who likes telling the truth, who stands up for herself . . . and who will no longer violate her standards of what feels right, in the interest of peace. I know I spent at least the first twenty-five years of my life in the first camp, and most of the second twenty-five years in the second camp. The problem is that "the new me" can tend to pull into overdrive in defense of her position. To the point that I only started contemplating that I might want to bring it down a notch when my basically exceptional partner told me (maybe around the eighty-seventh time), "I need you to give me some space to be human."

As both a recovering afraid-of-you-being-mad-at-me person and a therapist with an ear for the "incongruent" response, I could be murder to deal with at times (i.e., "*So, if you were feeling shut down, why couldn't you have immediately told me? Then you could be shut down AND we could have a relationship!*"). So, at a certain point, I really had to look at whether my being the Relationship Safety Patrol was truly caring for the relationship or managing my anxiety around connection and my fear of reverting to the old me.

If your partner holds up this message, take a moment to consider if your relational standards might have become a little too high (for example, maybe coming home to a cluttered house is just a sign your partner is tired and not a sign that he is totally oblivious to what matters to you). The partner who flashes this card is simply wanting your trust that he or she cares how you think and feel—but just needs a moment to breathe and exist before getting into the heavier stuff.

120.

I need to be able to
risk sharing my distrust
with you. It's the only
way I am ever going
to trust you.

I'd say that myths around "unconditional love" are responsible for a lot of relationship unhappiness. In the early days of a relationship, this, combined with the blindness associated with being crazy-in-love, can be a lethal combination. In my twenties I started dating a gorgeous Harvard-educated Prince Charming whose brother was a world-famous folk singer at the time, and the whole grown-up scene had me convinced for a week that I had finally transcended my history as a relationship loser. So besotted was I that when I saw that one of Prince Charming's checks had both his name and a female with the same last name on it, I innocently commented, "You have a checking account with your mother?" Okay, I was young, and these days an average sixteen-year-old would guess that he might have been married, but the point is that when we fall in love, the tendency is to idealize the object of our affections (e.g., *"Mom, can't you see? He doesn't have a job because sometimes deeply creative people need time to regroup"*).

But idealizing someone isn't trusting them, and the process of really and truly trusting someone requires having enough space in the relationship to share our occasionally inevitable moments of distrust. This can range anywhere from "I'm afraid if I don't lose the weight after the baby is born, you'll stop loving me," to "I know you don't want me to bring your past up again, but when I couldn't track you down at the motel, I had the scary thought that you might have been having a drink with a woman at the bar."

It is indeed hard for the innocent listener of these remarks to hear the vulnerability of the speaker—to hear these reality checks less as accusations and more as evidence of actual trust on the worrier's part that they could risk being vulnerably paranoid with you in the service of routing out lingering worry and little distortions that seem to be endemic to the human condition. A Receiver who can respond to this flash card by welcoming your distrust as trust-building will be seen as a very trustworthy friend.

121.

I want you to tell me when you are not trusting me. It's the only way you are ever going to trust me.

This is the companion card to the one preceding it. It's particularly useful when the Sender is a person known to be "in recovery" for some less-than-wonderful habit or pattern that justifiably elicited distrust in the past. This could be an obvious common addiction like substance abuse, pornography or gambling, but also for something they don't yet have twelve-step programs for . . . like: automatically calling your sister-in-law for advice before asking me . . . or not sticking to your low-glycemic prediabetic agreed-upon eating regimen . . . or telling me you absolutely asked your employer for a raise, when, in fact, you simply chickened out.

We all know these patterns don't change overnight, and it puts the "co-partner" in the position of wondering from time to time about their partner's follow-through and feeling mortally terrified of insulting them by suggesting that there might have been a little slippage. For the person who is wanting to rightfully earn back their partner's trust, the most beautiful and healing thing you can do—besides sincerely cleaning up your act—is giving your beloved space to have a paranoid, sub-trusting thought about you now and then. To me, "making amends," which is part of any good Recovery Process, should include acknowledging that my impact on you is not something that just happened in the past. If I know my bad pattern harmed you, then I need to know that even my commitment to newfound sobriety and/or sane living can't immediately undo how I've conditioned you to expect otherwise. And if I demand blind faith, then I am undermining the development of a deeper trust that needs time to germinate and blossom . . . and gently withstand a handful of upsetting, likely paranoid moments from the person who wants desperately to trust me.

122.

I know it's hard to trust
me when I've been so on
the fence about us.

Once upon a time in our culture, many "pre-married" people conformed to one or the other of the following stereotypes: the characters known as the girl who went to college to get her "MRS. degree" and "the commitment-phobic man." Nowadays, it's not for nothing that Facebook has a relationship category called "It's complicated."

Many relatively in-touch men and women will acknowledge that there are parts of them that are afraid of intimacy, afraid that they will lose their newly found Selves in a serious one-on-one relationship ("I've worked so hard to find out who I am" is a frequent refrain I hear from women, from, oh, I'd say, twenty-five to sixty-five, or "I'm afraid of getting stuck with someone who really isn't my soul mate," from men and women alike). And believe me, it gets über-complicated when two professionals who have each commuted a doable forty-five minutes each way to work now face the prospect that living together means that the one who has more "logistical flexibility" might now need to be doubling their travel time . . . or when you

are a woman raised assuming the man would be the breadwinner, and you're crazy about your partner—only he makes one-third the income that you do, and you wish it didn't bother you, but it does . . . or when you love your partner dearly but feel panicked about how her intensely loud fourteen-year-old son will impact your easily rattled six-year-old daughter. "Complicated" doesn't even do it justice. Managing relationships these days can feel like that category, "advanced complex brainteasers."

That being said, a distinction needs to be made between complexity and what has been commonly called "ambivalence." If your relationship really means something to you, and your partner wants to take the next step—whatever that is—and you've been giving vague or hard-to-decode mixed messages, it would be a trust-building next step to acknowledge your waffling has been trust-eroding. And it would be extremely courageous to be willing to simplify the self-protective brainteaser you have perpetuated.

123.

I know you feel awful—
but it's not enough.
I need you to really,
really know what
it was like for me.

Within the context of a relationship, when one partner's offense has been so piercing to the other's self-worth, self-image, and their basic template of trust, much of the Betrayed's energy can tend to go, unfortunately, into wanting the Betrayer to feel worse than they, the Betrayed, do. And the Betrayer does feel terrible. Unless they're a psychopath, a partner who loves you but has done something distinctly not above-board will usually be consumed with a guilt that is very, very hard to let go of. Particularly if you don't want them to.

But who wants a partner who behaves honorably because guilt is keeping them in line? In a relatively sane reparation process (remembering that "relatively" is the operative word here), there comes a turning point when the Victim no longer needs to manage their diminishment by making sure the Offender feels small. Surely, when a deceit is first revealed, the Victim wants and deserves the Offender to feel pretty miserable—but at a certain point, the Victim realizes there's no real nourishment in it . . . and the continuing reenactment of how-could-you-have-done-that-to-me? and how-could-I-have-done-that-to-you? produces a kind of stasis—if not boredom—of its own.

There is no amount of breast-beating, on one's knees apologizing—or, for that matter, harsh penance—that will melt the recovering Victim. Only when the Victim knows that you *know* what it was like for her not only enduring your specific act of poor character, but robbing her of her trust, of her sureness in feeling *he could never do that to me,* as well as at least temporarily robbing her of her ability to admire you, will you be able to stop apologizing for the old you and start living as the new you. And the person who can nonabrasively, nonsadistically say, "Your feeling awful just isn't enough," usually is a person who has regained her self-worth. Such a person would rather feel felt than torture you.

124.

It's hard to trust you
when you don't do what
you say you'll do.

This is a card where I think too much explanation on my part will undercut what should be axiomatic about this message. The only thing I'll add, risking implying that this, too, might not be obvious, is that taking ownership for a broken agreement or a task taken on that has been left undone can also be trust-building. But you'd better do it proactively . . . and soon.

125.

When you sound annoyed when I bring it up again, I feel I have to pretend I'm past it—and I'm not.

This is a flash card that really requires the Sender's discernment . . . and now that I think about it, the Receiver's maturity.

No one likes a nag, but some things don't go away in just one sitting. This card was NOT designed to give you license to drive someone crazy through hammering it to death, but to acknowledge the many situations where something so disturbing occurred—particularly a violation of trust—that who are we kidding to think we can have one grievance session with one heartfelt apology and think we are "complete"?

When a hurt person feels they are clearing things on borrowed time because their partner feels so badly hearing about it, this is where we end up with pseudocompletion.

And I promise you this will never lead to genuine harmony. I tell you, the three little words that can ultimately bring things to speedier completion better than just about anything are not "I love you," but "Is there more?"

So maybe it will help seeing it in print from a mental health professional who works a lot with couples: It is normal, appropriate and usually wholesome to tell someone more than once when they have deeply hurt us or violated what we have considered sacred. Only one note of caution: repeats work better when conducted with discernment and maturity . . . and the awareness the listener really *has* heard it before.

126.

Honey, I feel myself starting to get triggered. What can we do to move this in a different direction?

I'm sitting here staring at this statement, imagining what the world would be like today if every parent used some version of this message as soon as their kid started to make them feel unheard, annoyed or otherwise on the verge of losing it.

Imagine growing up in an environment where those in power took responsibility for their own pushed buttons, and turned these hot-button parent-child moments into invitations to collaborate with you—not just as an opportunity to pull rank. The lesson this would teach kids is: You have just as much ability as I do to create a more mutually satisfying interaction. I believe this would create a world pretty free of blame—where different agendas or timetables or even different values didn't automatically make us enemies.

The person who can feel triggered and still choose mutuality over emotional withdrawal is offering a level of friendship and sanity that, sadly, is not the norm on this planet. Memorize this message. While it might initially seem otherwise, it's actually more grounding, freeing and pro-relationship than making sure you don't trigger someone or protecting yourself from getting triggered, i.e., how you may well have spent the last two-thirds of your life.

127.

Before we go on,
first you have to tell
me you love me.

A couple of months ago a couple came into a session with me where the wife was extremely upset that in a restaurant with two other couples present, the husband had leaned over and whispered, "Honey, do you really need that second piece of bread? The meal will be here soon." I was empathic with the woman, who felt shamed and self-conscious, but, to be honest, the degree of her uproar also had me feeling empathic toward the husband, who felt he had bent over backward to be gentle, supportive of her presumed diet and unobtrusive. Usually in sessions, I'm good about getting partners away from "he said/she said," but for some reason I allowed a conversation to go on far too long about whether or not the husband had, in fact, "whispered" in the restaurant. Something was percolating in me. I stopped the action and told the husband to pretend we were in the restaurant and tell me exactly what he'd told his wife.

Modeling another way of handling his remark, I leaned forward and looked Mr. Diet Squad in the eye: "I have no idea whether I need the piece of bread or not," I told him, "but before I make any decision on the matter I need you to tell me I'm beautiful and that you will love me no matter what I weigh!"

I was modeling the way out, insisting upon loving oneself so much that it becomes next to impossible to absorb what might be hurtful in another's observations. I mean, think about it—you and your partner are having an unpleasant discussion about something. Could this flash card do anything but help? It could certainly slow down the action and likely optimize the chance that the two of you actually get to talk constructively about the issue at hand—rather than continuing to manage the underlying "does he (or she) value me enough?" issue indirectly, defensively and not as real friends. Use this flash card and everything else will fall into place in about ninety seconds.

This is what trusting *oneself* can look like. Sort of like: "*Talk to me like I'm someone you love.*" Sort of like dynamite.

Acknowledgments

Talk to Me Like I'm Someone You Love is the product of my lifelong quest to figure out what it means to be real, and how to bring that consciousness naturally into relationships. I would like to mention some special teachers who were there for me in my struggle, and who each patiently held space for me to arrive.

Roger Serota, a beautiful man who opened up for me the possibility of emotional safety.

Carolyn Tilove of the Philadelphia Pathwork, who demonstrated by personal example that you never have to pretend.

Shirley Luthman, whose brilliant book *Collection* was pivotal in helping me organize my own thinking about staying in relationship with oneself.

Larry Kaiden, who trusted in my ability to flow when I felt anything but "flow-y."

Ted Strauss, whose profound trust in Beingness and enormous heart allowed me to fall into the paradox of neither denying brokenness nor believing anything needed to be fixed.

Along with Ted, I want to acknowledge some other members of the Waking Down in Mutuality teaching community who have shown me much about falling into the Self: Hillary Davis, who had a fierce commitment to my awakening; Krishna Gauci, Sandra Glickman,

Cielle Backstrom, Dan Will and founder Saniel Bonder, a master of conscious embodiment whose commitment to others being true to themselves is wondrous. Though not a formal Waking Down teacher, my dear friend Peggy Tobin has provided ongoing support of both a tender and metaphysical nature. And Deborah Boyar, Ph.D., has been the most remarkable combination of girlfriend and sage.

I also wish to acknowledge:

Michael Gerber, CEO of E-Myth International, who sat across from me years ago at Café Beaujolais in Mendocino and declared, "It's a book!"

My father, William Greenberg, for supporting my return to graduate school, and my mother, Eloise Greenberg, for her intense interest in what makes people tick.

Talk to Me's midwives:

Meredith Gould, dear and brainy, who first put *Flash Cards for Real Life* on the map. Lea Belair, a master coach whose fundamental sense of How Things Are allowed me to take my inner journey into the world. Jan Friedman, whose clarity of vision, basic sharpness and gentle insistence allowed me to enlarge the destination. The brother-sister team of Paul Weiner and Geralyn Lucas, whose enthusiastic support and true care provided several bridges to make the destination real.

Scott Laserow, a graphic genius, website designer and total mensch, whose devotion to this project inspired me more than he knows.

Joelle Delbourgo, a wonderful agent, who time and again showed me the place where realistic and idealistic don't have to cancel each other out.

Sara Carder, my amazing editor at Tarcher, whose grasp of the nuances of relationship, common sense and utter kindness managed to make this book more earthbound and heavenbound than it could ever have been without her.

Susan Harrow, whose refined consciousness, naturalness and stunning decency turn media coaching into a path of enlightenment.

Rob Dreyfus, stepson and human being extraordinaire.

Bob Dreyfus, beautiful ex-husband, who, despite everything, still trusted that gentleness was the truth about me.

Barbara Hastings, a girlfriend in a class of her own, whose clarity, spaciousness and pure love have healed more in me than words can say.

Matthew Cohen, a special friend, whose integrity, wisdom and loving willingness to ask, "Is there more?" allowed me to test-drive much of what I hoped to be true.

Kim and Jack Linder, whose love, sincerity and sanity have always been a breath of fresh air.

Hannah Grace and Eric Grace are to be acknowledged just for Being Who They Are . . . no matter what.

Tim Wentz, whose love and grace have allowed me to walk my talk . . . and has kept me speechless.

And all those additional people who, by their very natures, have led me at different times in my life to deeper places of truth: Craig Aaron, Alix Amar, Beverly Bright, John and Jessica Cioci, Ellen Cohen, Rachel Cohen, Shelia Coleman, Hillary Costin, Hale Dwoskin, Patricia Kirsten Ehrmann, Mary Fahy, Bronwyn Falcona, Nedra Fetterman, Ilene Gerber, Meredith Henry Geringer, Mignon Groch, Edye Kamensky, Amanda Owen, Ginny Rials, Lisa Rogers, Abby Sandler, the late Ernie Schier, Sunny Shulkin, Lenn Snyder, Ralph S. Sterling, Ann Strong, Judy Watson, Paul Weiner, Esther Melmed Weiss, Sylvia Woods and Lisagail Zeitlin.

My final acknowledgment is to my daughter, Carly, who, just under five years old, took a Magic Marker and made up her first flash card: "MOMMY U STOP IT." She said, "It's for when your mommy's mad or when she's at the computer and you want her to play."

YOUR OWN PERSONAL FLASH

CARDS FOR REAL LIFE

· *Create Your Own Flash Card* ·

· *Create Your Own Flash Card* ·

· Create Your Own Flash Card ·

· *Create Your Own Flash Card* ·

· Create Your Own Flash Card ·

Create Your Own Flash Card

· *Create Your Own Flash Card* ·

· *Create Your Own Flash Card* ·